COLD-
BLOODED
MURDER

COLD-BLOODED MURDER

WHEN PEARL GAMBLE REJECTED ROBERT McGLADDERY, LUST TURNED TO RAGE. THIS IS THE TRUE STORY OF HER CRUEL, VICIOUS MURDER.

PATRICK GREG

JOHN BLAKE

Published by John Blake Publishing Ltd,
3 Bramber Court, 2 Bramber Road,
London W14 9PB, England

www.johnblakepublishing.co.uk

First published in paperback in 2010

ISBN 978 1 84454 843 9

British Library Cataloguing-in-Publication Data:

A catalogue record for this book is available from the British Library.

Design by www.envydesign.co.uk

Printed and bound in Great Britain by CPI Bookmarque,
Croydon CR0 4TD

1 3 5 7 9 10 8 6 4 2

Papers used by John Blake Publishing are natural, recyclable products made
from wood grown in sustainable forests. The manufacturing processes
conform to the environmental regulations of the country of origin.

Every attempt has been made to contact the relevant copyright-holders,
but some were unobtainable. We would be grateful if the appropriate
people could contact us.

In memory of Dorothy Hill

ACKNOWLEDGEMENTS

Thanks to Greg and Ellie for turning the volume down on the telly every now and again, and to my wife Heather for shutting the door tight. To my mum for her biased criticism and to Michael and Billy for pointing me in the right direction in the first place. A general nod to anyone else who helped me out along the way by sharing their own recollections.

© Sole Syndication · © Belfast Telegraph

Robert McGladdery and his victim, Pearl Gamble

CONTENTS

INTRODUCTION

In Northern Ireland the period from 1970 until the end of the Nineties saw the slaughter of many innocent men, women and children, often day after day. Murder and mayhem became a way of life for many living in the Province, the 'Troubles' churning out murderers by the dozen, each hiding behind one idealism or another in an attempt to validate their actions. At times the conflict that raged throughout this little backwater seemed to dominate the headlines of the world press. Throughout those years there were still instances of domestic murders, but they seldom made the front page of any newspaper or magazine. Back in 1961, however, just a few years before the situation in Northern Ireland featured on news bulletins all around the globe, you couldn't have lifted a local newspaper without reading the name Robert McGladdery.

It is a fact, uncomfortable though it may be, that we are obsessed with perpetrators of crimes of all sorts, particularly those who have taken a human life. Murder remains the ultimate taboo in the 'civilised' world, and our fascination with peering into the more bizarre and disturbing aspects of the murderer's mind feeds such industries as film, television and book publishing. Often the very people who commit murder do so in order to elevate their persona from that of a two-dimensional nobody to a complex and fathomless someone whose name will be remembered for ever, albeit for the wrong reasons. For others, though, it is either the sheer brutality of their act, or acts in the case of serial killers, which may raise their profile, so that their names will be listed alongside those of Bundy, Manson and Sutcliffe. Yet ask who their victims were, and sadly there will be few people able to answer.

In this respect the story of the last man to be hanged in Northern Ireland is no different. It involves a particularly cruel and horrific murder, details of which will be revealed in this book, and a killer who, it appears, sought some form of recognition. There is no question in my mind that the right man went to the gallows on that fateful day in December 1961, and I am sure that at the end of this book you will reach the same conclusion. The evidence presented to the court during his initial trial and subsequent appeal is conclusive. The sad truth in this story, as in others, is that many of us will instantly know his name but struggle to recall his victim. By rights, only the name of Pearl Gamble should come easily to our lips. After all, this is Pearl's story, even though I know she would not have wished such notoriety thrust upon her. It is she alone who deserves to be remembered, not the person who robbed her of her youth in such a cold-blooded manner. By rights her story should be a celebration of her life from babe to blossoming young woman. But in truth Pearl's life was unremarkable, and probably would have remained so. Unfortunately, we become acquainted with her only when she falls prey to a deluded and self-obsessed killer whose name lives on, while Pearl Gamble remains fresh in the memory only of those who knew and loved her.

There was an overwhelming innocence about the 19-year-old girl whose photograph stared back from the pages of the *Newry Reporter*. She had an engaging smile, and exuded youth and vitality, but she was very much the girl-next-door. How then had she become the victim of so heinous a crime? What was it about Pearl Gamble that had driven her killer into such a frenzy, inflicting upon her body the most horrific injuries, which, when described during the murder trial later that year, would test the resolve of some of the jurors? The answer, when it eventually came, was that Pearl had simply rejected the advances of one young man, and that rejection was something which Robert Andrew McGladdery could not accept.

Pearl was a war baby, and had lived with her mother and father at Upper Damolly in Newry with her three sisters and one brother. The family had lived there for nearly 30 years and Pearl had attended nearby Rockvale School until she was 15. On leaving Rockvale, having earned a scholarship, she spent a year at Newry Technical College. A popular figure during her time there, Pearl acquired a fairly large circle of friends both male and female, many of whom followed her into full-time employment as soon as they could. Jobs were hard to find at the time, but to Pearl's credit she secured a position in Foster Newell's furnishing and drapery store in the town on 20 October 1957, when she was still just 16. She quickly made a good impression on her employers and in October 1960 was given more responsibility and elevated to the status of a buyer in the material department, which brought her a fairly respectable monthly wage of £16. It was certainly a far cry from working on the factory floor at the Damolly Mill, but it wasn't the most glamorous job in the world either, and I am sure Pearl had dreams of one day marrying, having children and a good husband who would provide for the family. In that respect, and many others, she was like any other girl her age. Her sister Elizabeth had already been married off, but with her three other sisters – Marina then 25, Margaret 23 and Eleanor only just 14 – and her 21-year-old brother Robin still at home, finding her own space would have been difficult. No matter how happy a home she came from Pearl would have dreamed of having her own place with her own things around her, and realistically the only way that would happen would be by settling down with a partner.

By all accounts that was not going to be too long, as Pearl was a popular girl with the young men of the town. Popular because she was, of course, attractive, but also because of her fun-loving nature and her keen sense of humour. According to one of her friends, Evelyn Gamble (no relation of Pearl), she kept company with several young policemen from the local station. But, Evelyn stressed, Pearl was not into 'fooling around' and had at one time told her that if anyone ever touched her she would 'use her shoe on them and wouldn't leave a hair on their head'. Pearl was certainly a feisty character and, as any young single woman was entitled to do, kept her options open.

Another of her friends, Rae Boyd, had witnessed someone attempting to 'get fresh' with Pearl one evening during the summer of 1960. A young man had taken

Pearl and Rae out in his car along with a friend of his. Rae and the man's friend had paired off in the back seat, while Pearl was in the front with her companion. At the end of the evening, when he stopped outside Pearl's house, he had hung on to her, preventing her from leaving the car for about five minutes. Rae described Pearl's reaction to what was likely to have been mere playfulness as 'frantic'. It was clear that Pearl could flirt just the same as anyone else, but she had strict rules of what was permitted and what wasn't.

For Pearl and other young people in and around Newry the main social scene was a visit to one of the many coffee shops dotted around the town, where they would catch up with friends and pump coins into the jukebox. But what they all looked forward to most was the weekends.

In the North and the Republic alike at the end of the Fifties and into the Sixties, dancehalls and ballrooms enjoyed a golden era which will never be forgotten by those who are lucky enough to count themselves among their patrons in those days. There was a genuine buzz about at the time, with teenagers embracing the music and their newfound freedom with vigour. Many of them had experienced the war years as young children, and had watched their mothers and fathers struggling with rationing, unemployment and the uncertainty that the conflict had brought with it. Now, though, it was their time, and their optimism was infectious. They could see a new and exciting future lying ahead of them, and they fully intended to make the most of it. Out went the grey days of hand-me-down clothes and smuggled butter and eggs, and along came tight dresses, Teddy boys and rock 'n' roll. Dotted across all Ireland were hundreds of dancehalls, and even more smaller venues like pubs, clubs and parochial halls, where weekly dances flourished. It was to just such venues that the great show bands of the time were to draw large crowds of young men and women, and eventually turn a somewhat lacklustre music scene on its end, in turn earning themselves almost iconic status.

The audiences in the early Fifties had been used to large orchestral-type bands with 10 or 12 seated musicians conducted by a bandleader. The music they played was current, but there was nothing inspirational about the performance. Along came the show bands, and with some quite ordinary singers up front and the musicians moving with more enthusiasm than real rhythm as they played to the crowd, the dances took on a new meaning.

Of course there were big names in the show band circuit, like Brendan Bowyer, Dickie Rock and Joe Dolan, and should they ever come to town, anyone who could either get a ticket, or bribe their way into the venue, did so. Teenagers would scour the local newspapers each week checking venues like St Colman's Parochial Hall to find out who was coming next and when. Acts such as the Galway-based show band The Capitol and Belfast's Avonaires still played church halls and were renowned for putting on a great night's entertainment regardless of how insignificant the surroundings. But, to their credit, the locals also supported the lesser-known acts who regularly played the sports clubs and bingo halls in towns and villages across the country, and it was these young musicians who provided the music for dances week-in and week-out without fail. Often they were local lads who could hold a tune, accompanied by a small band more than willing to receive payment in the form of a pint or two, with the adoration of the local females being an added bonus.

In the dimmed lights suspended overhead, the girls, full-figured and coiffed, would eye up the lads for a possible match and take to the floor as many times as they were asked. The more seasoned male campaigners would pose at the opposite side of the hall in sharp suits, cloaked in cigarette smoke and reeking of beer, waiting for the opportunity to pounce on those girls left unattached at the end of the evening. On occasion, when the venue was a church hall, the parish priest or minister might choose to preside over the evening's entertainment, keeping a sharp eye on anything deemed remotely inappropriate. Alcohol was banned from many dances, but where there was a will there was a way, and many would slip outside briefly to take a pull from a well-hidden bottle or two. Generally the dances were good-natured, with the odd bloody nose or broken heart being the only casualties. Everyone was there to enjoy the music and dance away the night, leaving any inhibitions or minor disagreements to the side.

On one such night, however, and in just such a dancehall, a different dynamic was at work. The events that followed would change the lives of many forever and rock the foundations of a small community to its core.

By today's standards the Sixties were an age of relative innocence for most, especially those living in rural parts of both Northern Ireland and the Republic. Never quite falling in step with mainland Britain, always slightly behind the trends of the time, people lived a much simpler existence. There were still many areas where electricity had yet to reach, with oil lamps and coal fires the only source of light and heat for thousands. The pace of life moved much more slowly, and most were content that it did, adamant that change was not always for the better. Many young people growing up in Ireland during the post-war years frequently strayed to England or further afield in search of employment. Others, either less ambitious or lucky enough to secure a career or job in local established businesses or industry, never moved more than a few miles from where they were born.

In smaller towns and villages everyone knew each other's business, and if they didn't, it was not long before they did. Families throughout country areas were often related in one way or another to their neighbours for miles around, and both good and bad news travelled faster than the newspapers could ever dream of delivering it. But the 'jungle telegraph', as it was often called, appeared to bring bad news to the doorstep more swiftly than good. I'll always remember my paternal grandmother and her tales of woe when my parents would bring me and my brother back to the family home in Portadown to visit her. We would have been in the house hardly five minutes when she would start to reel off names of the recently departed from around the town or the little rural communities stretching out towards the shores of Lough Neagh, where she herself had grown up. She was a walking obituary column. Likewise, on her own untimely demise, relatives whose names I had never heard mention of before, hailing from God knows where, arrived at the family home to pay their respects. The news of her passing had reached far and wide, and the jungle telegraph had once again spread the bad news with an enviable efficiency. That was the way it was for people of her generation.

It stood to reason, then, that news of a murder in a small town would have spread throughout the community like wildfire, and even more so when the details which emerged painted the picture of a brutal and frenzied attack on an innocent young woman. And that was how it was, when on Saturday, 28 January 1961, the body of a young Newry shop girl, Pearl Gamble, was found slain and concealed from sight amid gorse bushes near the sparsely populate rural area of Damolly in County Down.

One young boy, who at that time had a somewhat vested interest in the Gamble family in the form of his adoration for one of Pearl's younger sisters, was later to describe, in an essay published in the *Newry Journal*, the awful events of that morning, and just how much they would impact on him and his community. John McCullagh, who was 13 at the time, had set his sights on one 'stunningly beautiful brown-eyed girl', whom he had seen talking with her older sister in Foster Newell's department store in Hill Street. Although he was not alone among his peers in developing an interest in young women, he still described himself as an oddball, spending all his money on the *New Musical Express* and immersing himself in the pop music of the time which was brought to him through the family's wireless radio. As it was for most people then, it would be years before he owned a television, and radio was the only real link to the great big world outside. Still, through radio, the influences of modern-day Britain managed to seep into small, insular communities, where, when television did eventually make an appearance, it was described by many, including McCullagh himself, as an 'intrusion'.

Even the street games children played were self-made and involved some sort of craft or ingenuity. One such game, called Kaddy, which was played at the kerb, was a favourite of John and his friends. An oblong piece of wood, sharpened at both ends and with each of its four faces numbered one to four, was struck with a rod to toss it high into the air. If the 'kaddy' was caught, the player who had hit it was 'out' and the catcher was 'in'. If not, the number which faced upwards when it landed determined how many strokes you were left when you were 'in'.

It was while playing Kaddy outside his front door on that sunny January morning that John remembers the bread delivery man, Michael Campbell, going from door to door imparting his terrible news. John and his friends would not have normally taken any notice of Campbell, nor he of them, only something about his behaviour struck the boys as being different. For a start he was late. But much more than that, his behaviour was 'animated'. As they followed Campbell from house to house, it soon became clear that something awful had happened to Pearl Gamble, and that the person who was thought to have done it was Robert McGladdery.

John McCullagh describes the aftermath of the events of that day as 'the end of our innocence; and not just for us, but for our sleepy backwater of a town as well'. His powerful words 'end of our innocence' sum up, I believe, the effect Pearl Gamble's murder had on the community and underscore its importance in shaping Newry's rural society in the early Sixties.

Although I was born after the event, in 1962, some of my earliest memories of my own home town of Bangor, in County Down, are similar to McCullagh's. The games we played in the garden or the street were virtually all of our own making, with few if any props required. If we were lucky and weather permitting, during holidays we were taken to Pickie Pool for the afternoon, an open-air seawater swimming pool where the water was always cold but never empty of bathers. That or a jaunt in one of Laird's rowing boats around the harbour or a trip to the Copeland Islands was usually more than you could hope for. What summers we had when I was a young boy were long and hot, or at least seemed so, and were mostly spent on one beach or another, jumping the waves, building sandcastles or playing cricket and football. The winters almost always brought snowfalls which prompted us to improvise a sled from a few scraps of wood and take it to the slopes of the Valentine playing fields beside our local park.

It was one particular holiday I spent at my great aunt's little cottage on the shores of Lough Neagh when I was five or maybe six which is one of my earliest and fondest memories. The cottage was tiny and sat at the very end of a long lane which was only the width of a car and full of cavernous potholes. There were only two bedrooms, as far as I can remember, and a door leading off from the kitchen opened directly into a hayshed. The water came from a pump across the way from the front door, and the lean-to beside it housed an ancient old tractor and a stump where wood for the fire was cut with an axe. My memories of those few days are filled with magic: stories told around the turf fire burning in the grate in the evening, and board games played on the little dining table until nearly midnight. The days were a mixture of jumping around in the haystacks or wandering through the fields and watching while the turf was being cut and piled up to dry at the side. There was an abundance of fresh air, and a tranquillity which was never interrupted by anything other than the bark of a dog or the song of a bird.

Many of us will remember scenes like these, and recall just how insulated from the outside world the small rural communities were, much more so than the likes of seaside tourist towns such as Bangor could be. I can well understand how the events of 28 January 1961 had a catastrophic impact on some of those living in and around Newry. The murder of Pearl Gamble brought with it a realisation that bad things could happen even there in the midst of their own little world, where people seldom locked their front doors and many thought nothing of walking home along the unlit roads and lanes on the darkest of winter nights.

It is a sad indictment of the society we live in today that we have become so accustomed to stories of violence and murder reported in the media that we hardly give it a second thought. In turn, I realise that the story of one murder which happened almost half a century ago will therefore have even less significance to many of us now, unless you can grasp just how much the world has changed over that time.

Try to imagine your world without colour television and only two channels to watch anyway, should you be lucky enough to have an electricity supply. Consider regularly having to negotiate horse-drawn vehicles in your path as you drive your less-than-streamlined motor car along pitted and potholed B-roads as you travel to a job which pays wages in pounds, shillings and pence. Forget motorways: Britain's first, the M1, wasn't opened until 1964. Air travel was for the very rich and destinations very limited at that, and foreign holidays were the stuff of dreams. For most of us, Butlins or the west of Ireland were as exotic as it got. Fast food was always fish and chips, and a 'Chinese' or 'Indian' just meant someone from the other side of the world.

If you can imagine living a life as simple as this, you

may begin to appreciate how the savagery of Pearl Gamble's murder managed to permeate the lives of so many and bring a very unwelcome awakening.

CHAPTER ONE

MISSING

Newry was elevated to city status in March 2002 as part of Queen Elizabeth's Golden Jubilee celebrations. With an ever-growing population, today topping 35,000, it is a far cry from its early-20th-century identity. The centre of Newry straddles the Clanrye River, which marks the historic border between County Down and County Armagh, and the town hall, under which the river runs, commands an imposing position looking towards the entrance to the main shopping area of Hill Street.

The town was established in 1144 with the construction of a monastery, and over the next few hundred years grew in size owing to its prominent position at the entrance to the Gap of the North, the most accessible road between Northern Ireland and the Republic, and its development as a market town.

Unfortunately most of Newry was burnt to the ground by the retreating forces of King James II in 1689 as he made his way south in an attempt to outrun William III, but the subsequent rebuilding programme provided the basis for the town's emergence as one of the busiest ports in Ulster. The fact that the town lay more or less midway between Belfast and Dublin was significant, to say the least, and it soon became an important centre of trade, with the linen industry in particular bringing much-needed employment to the local workforce in the late 19th century and indeed until recent times. Through the early part of the 20th century there were thriving mills in Drumalane, Bessbrook and Damolly, each employing generation after generation of families whose offspring were destined to leave school at around 15 years of age. A second level of education was only affordable to middle-class families of some substance, and they were few and far between.

In the Forties and Fifties Newry expanded little beyond Kilmorey Street and Monaghan Street, with little dots of town land lying at its greenfield fringes. Times were hard, and Newry saw many emigrate to the United States in search of a new life. There was an underlying uncertainty both politically and commercially, particularly in the late Fifties, and many people weren't quite sure when things would stabilise, if ever.

Unluckily for Newry, lying so close to the Irish Republic, it featured heavily in the IRA's late-Fifties border campaign. Targets for the IRA bombers included Victoria Locks and the town's Civil Service office, which incorporated the Employment Exchange. Some nineteen attacks were carried out, each aimed at places or people who it appeared had links, however tenuous, with British imperialism. Newry's reputation as a quiet town was being damaged by the adverse publicity. At one point in 1957 the Minister of Home Affairs, Colonel W.W.B. Topping, imposed a late-night curfew on the inhabitants in response to the rise in terrorist activity. According to the rules of curfew, everyone who had not obtained an official permit from the Royal Ulster Constabulary, or RUC, would not be allowed on the streets between 11pm and 5am. Emergency services were, of course, exempt, as were clergy and some journalists.

Scores of officers from the Ulster Special Constabulary, known as 'B Specials', were deployed to break up any resistance to the curfew, but even so, many people were willing to run the gauntlet. Among those to voice their anger at the implementation of what seemed an archaic approach to the maintenance of public order, was Max Keogh, then Chairman of Newry Council. According to Keogh, he was speaking for the majority of Newry citizens, whatever their religious persuasion, when he demanded that the liberty of the townspeople be restored, characterising the curfew as 'a most drastic step'. Eventually the curfew was lifted, but the 'frontier' town, as some had described it, warranted the retention of numerous Special Constables in case any further insurgency got out of hand.

There may have been some turbulent times in Newry's recent history, and the Fifties certainly rated among them, but a great sense of community still remained. Despite the influence of the train link with Ireland and the constant improvement of the local infrastructure during the late Fifties and early Sixties, the town retained a very rural aspect.

Situated in a tight-knit little area of South Down, Newry was in short a thriving provincial shopping town but with a strong village mentality. It is no surprise then that Pearl Gamble, or for that matter Robert McGladdery, was known to many of its inhabitants. After all, it wasn't a big place, and at that time religion was not enough of an issue to seriously divide the community.

A local journalist who grew up in Newry in the late Fifties and early Sixties, although agreeing that there were very few episodes of blatant sectarianism that he could remember, did tell me that there were very defined areas of the town where the Nationalist and Unionist communities lived separately, albeit fairly harmoniously. He described the reason for this division as one of practicality more than anything else. From my own experiences of the town in the early Eighties, I do remember the area around the Belfast Road as being predominantly Protestant, while others, including Derrybeg, then on the outskirts of Newry, was clearly Nationalist. But, speaking to other people who were teenagers during the Sixties and came from opposing communities within the Newry area, I found that their memories were different. They recalled having a wider circle of friends encompassing all denominations, with some young Catholic and Protestant men and women not only socialising together but often dating one another and sometimes forming lasting relationships. As the more liberal influence of the Sixties took hold, old attitudes were challenged and young people began to mix more readily, shaking off age-old fears and suspicions.

One such opportunity for them to come together came in the form of a Friday-night dance held in the Henry Thompson Memorial Orange Hall and organised by the Newry Girl Guide Rangers. The Orange Hall, as it was known, was situated on the main Belfast Road and the caretaker, John Albert Wilson, and his wife Maud, who lived on the premises, had made preparations for what they knew would be a busy night. Although the dance wouldn't be in full swing until after 11, coinciding with kicking-out time at the local pubs, the band still had to set up, and John Wilson eventually opened the doors to the hall at around nine o'clock that evening.

All across the town preparations were being made for the big night out. Girls were fussing with their make-up and picking out a suitable skirt or dress, while the boys tried to match a tie to the only shirt which was ironed. Pearl Gamble had left ample time to prepare herself, and had chosen a tight-fitting grey skirt with a white blouse and a black knitted jumper. For it was January, cold and damp, and she intended to walk to the dance with her two friends, Rae Boyd and Evelyn Gamble. The three of them were all shop assistants and would have had plenty to talk about during the three-quarters of an hour it would take to get there.

Rae and Evelyn arrived for Pearl at around 9.30 that evening and chatted for around 15 minutes as Pearl made the last little adjustments to her hair and clothes and finished a chapter in a book she had been reading. Like many of the girls, Pearl would walk to the dance in one pair of shoes while carrying another pair which were purely for dancing. When they eventually left the house, at around 9.45, they bade Mrs Gamble good night and started out on their walk. This would be the last time Margaret Gamble would see her daughter alive.

On the morning of Saturday, 28 January 1961, a few hours after the dance at the Orange Hall, 16-year-old Charles Ashe took his greyhounds out to exercise them, as he often did. At around 8.50, as he walked on

Primrose Hill towards the old Damolly Road, he noticed a black shoe lying in the centre of the entrance into Weir's field. Without thinking, Ashe lifted the shoe and tossed it into the hedgerow to his right a few yards ahead. When he walked on again he saw other items lying on the ground, in particular a black scarf and a silk scarf, both to his right, the silk scarf in a water channel in the drain, the black scarf in the ditch beside it. Then he quickly spotted a pair of brown shoes and another black shoe. One of the brown shoes was lying beside a pair of gloves and a piece of paper, also beside the hedge, while the other lay in the middle of the road.

All these items were less than five yards away from what was known as the Upper Damolly crossroads, and only a few hundred yards from the home of Margaret Gamble and her family. Charles Ashe was not able to say definitively, when questioned later by the police, whether or not he had touched any of the other items, but he felt sure that he hadn't. He had no reason to suspect anything untoward, and he continued his walk, turning left at the crossroads and heading towards the Belfast Road. Before long he noticed a bicycle lying behind the hedge in the field to his left, and further along he came across Bob McCullough, a farm labourer, who was fixing the gates leading into the same field. McCullough remarked to Ashe that he had noticed that there were bicycle tracks going through the gap in the mud and continuing into the field, but neither of them thought much more about it.

McCullough had been working on the gates since 7.45 that morning, and had ridden his own bicycle up to the field from his home at Cloughenrammer. In need of some brute force to complete his job, about 20–30 minutes after Ashe had passed, McCullough climbed on his bike and made his way to the top of Primrose Hill, where he had left a sledgehammer the previous evening. As he turned right into the start of the hill he noticed female clothing and shoes lying across the road, and further on, a shoe on top of the ditch. He rode on, and when he reached the spot at the top of the hill where he had been working the previous day, he looked in vain for the sledgehammer.

As he rode back down the hill towards the crossroads McCullough stopped the bike to have a closer look at the bits and pieces strewn across his path. They lay very much where Ashe had seen them, but on looking more closely, McCullough saw what appeared to be a dried blood stain on one of the scarves. His instinct was not to touch any of the items, but instead he continued to look around and make a visual note of where they were. In doing so he also noted a 'smoothed out' spot in the ditch where it looked as if two people had stood for a while. McCullough had seen enough, and as the rain started to fall he made his way down towards Margaret Gamble's house to tell her what he had found.

It was routine for Mrs Gamble to wake and rise at 5am in order to get one of her daughters up and out to work at the Damolly Mill. She had retired to bed at 1.30am, choosing not to wait up for Pearl but instead leaving a candle and matches on the table for her return. After all, she knew the dance would finish late and it would take the girls some time to get a lift home. Pearl had never given her any cause for concern; she was a sensible girl. But, when she checked the bedroom, and her daughter's bed, it was obvious she hadn't come back. When she spoke to reporters later that day Margaret Gamble said that she hadn't been unduly worried, as she had thought Pearl may have stayed the night at the home of one of her female friends.

But when Bob McCullough called at her door that morning and told her what he had found just yards from the crossroads, she must already have known deep down that Pearl was in trouble. It took her no time at all to follow McCullough up the road to the spot where the clothes lay. Pearl's younger sister Eleanor went with her mother and watched as she picked up the items, placed them under her arm and took them back to the house. Margaret Gamble had no idea that she was disturbing vital evidence in a crime scene. As far as she was concerned, she was retrieving items of clothing belonging to her daughter. Then both she and Eleanor left the house once more and walked up Primrose Hill again, further this time, still with McCullough. When they reached the gap into Weir's field he pointed out the black shoe to her, and she took this too. But it was only when Eleanor entered the field and returned a short time later with a handbag, that both she and her mother realised continuing looking for other items would be a mistake, and they hurried back home.

McCullough then mounted his bicycle and rode further along to Agnes Copeland's house, where he knew that there was a private telephone. When he told her of the discovery, she telephoned the RUC station in Newry without delay. It was now about 9.30.

That day the station orderly was Constable Robert Bamford, and as he took details from Agnes Copeland he must have considered that the circumstances warranted immediate action and made a report directly to Head Constable O'Hara.

Until recent years a Head Constable in a rural town such as Newry might well have had little in the way of major incidents to investigate. But the border campaign being waged by the IRA at the time was providing many challenges for even the most seasoned of police officers. On the very same day that Pearl and her friends were attending the dance in Newry, further west in the Province, near Roslea in County Fermanagh, a 26-year-old RUC officer was brutally murdered as he walked across the border into the Irish Republic to visit his girlfriend. Shot 15 times in the back with a submachine gun, Norman Anderson paid the ultimate price for serving the Crown. Widespread condemnation from both sides of the border could not detract from the fact that the border counties suffered worse than others simply because of their geography. Gunmen and murderers repeatedly found sanctuary in the Republic after escaping across a border that was proving impossible to physically define or police.

O'Hara and people like him had their work cut out for them, and by all accounts he was a particularly competent policeman, and an intuitive one. The brief details supplied by Bamford prompted him to rally other police officers, in particular Detective Sergeant Knox, to attend the Gambles' house as soon as possible. They arrived at around 9.45, just 15 minutes after the report of the crime was received.

On entering the house O'Hara and the others were shown the items that Mrs Gamble and her daughter had collected, all laid out on the kitchen floor. From his statement it is clear that Margaret Gamble had also found a coat, a skirt, a pair of panties and a black belt. Along with the items from the handbag were a hairbrush and a comb. Almost all of the belongings Pearl had taken out with her the previous evening lay on the floor. Knowing the value of a chain of evidence, O'Hara seized them all and attached identifying marks to each. He was now confident that this was a serious incident: a rape and assault, or worse.

The subtle differences between police procedure of those times and today can be seen in the marking of the exhibits as they appear on the various statements of evidence. O'Hara starts off with the clothes as pointed out to him in the Gambles' kitchen and gives the first item (a pair of black, stiletto-heeled shoes) the exhibit letter A. The next item (a pair of flat-heeled brown shoes) was marked as exhibit B, and so on. Regardless of which officer seized an item, he managed to mark it with the next letter in the alphabet until all 26 letters were exhausted. In those days, if there were further exhibits to be seized, they were identified as AA, AB, AC and so on, until this sequence was complete. After that it moved to BA, BB and so on. This was probably a fairly successful method of labelling items, but the chain of identification had to be kept tight. Today the opportunity to make mistakes numerically and chronologically is lessened as each individual officer recovering items of evidential value marks each item with his initials and a number, which in my case would be PG1, PG2 and so on.

As the rain began to fall more heavily outside, O'Hara made his way out of the house and back down towards the crossroads, where he spoke with Bob McCullough, asking him to point out where the items had first been spotted. Both men stopped just a few yards into the Old Damolly Road, and McCullough first showed O'Hara the disturbed earth on the bank. O'Hara noted the marks and similar ones just about three feet away on the same bank. To him it seemed obvious that some sort of struggle had taken place there. After McCullough had shown him the spot where the clothes had lain, and then the bicycle which lay behind the hedge in Weir's field, there was no doubt in his mind what had to be done.

A search was quickly organised for the missing girl, O'Hara having decided to concentrate efforts on the area around the Old Damolly Road, and in particular Weir's field. As an experienced policeman he was well aware that, should the incident turn out to involve a murder, time was of the essence. Not only because of the need to establish the facts as quickly as possible, but also because the rain which had strengthened while he had been carrying out his initial enquiries had the potential to destroy certain forensic evidence. A police dog was brought along to assist the searchers, but as with any coordinated search, it had to be undertaken at a snail's pace so that no vital clue would be overlooked.

At this stage Pearl Gamble was only considered 'missing', and despite the apparent blood on the scarf, nothing was being taken for granted. For all they knew, she could be lying injured somewhere, or being held against her will. They were making no assumptions.

The search had not long begun when, around 10.30am, DS Knox made a grim discovery, which he immediately relayed to O'Hara. Close to the head of Weir's field, about 30 yards from the gates, he had found a button and a bloodstained handkerchief, both of them lying on the grass, which itself showed signs of blood. Then, about 90 yards further on, towards the rise of the hill, he had found another patch of grass where a 'considerable' amount of blood staining was visible. O'Hara briefly stopped the search and made sure that both areas were covered in order to preserve evidence from the driving rain.

The field was fairly easy to search with the naked eye in that it was a stubble field, so that any disturbance in the soil, or any items lying around, were more readily spotted. Knox was also able to point out two left footprints prominent in the mud, and a piece of paper which appeared to be an insurance quotation.

Both O'Hara and Knox now believed they were dealing with a murder and that soon they would find Pearl's body.

Meanwhile the newspapers had got wind of the search for the missing girl and reports quoted a police spokesman who stressed that they were keeping an open mind in the matter even though they had found bloodstained clothing.

The search continued throughout the day, with the

small group of policemen making their way painstakingly across the field and the surrounding area. But it wasn't until 4.50 that afternoon that everyone's fears became a reality. As Special Constable Edward Bowers made his way slowly along a sheep track heading in the direction of the Belfast Road, he moved closer to a thick clump of gorse to investigate and saw a girl's body lying in a small clearing inside the bush. The body had been concealed just enough to hide it from the casual passer-by. Bowers stopped dead, then sent an urgent message to District Inspector Samuel Bradley, the most senior police officer on the ground at that time. They had found Pearl.

Inspector Bradley had joined the search at Damolly at about two o'clock that afternoon, fully aware that all hands would be needed when the ground to cover was potentially so large. When news of the find reached him at 4.55 he quickly made his way over to the place known locally as Weir's Rocks.

A seasoned police officer, Bradley immediately assessed the situation, and before anything else, established that life was extinct. There was no doubt that Pearl was dead. Her body was cold, lifeless and naked, save for her stockings. She lay face down in a prone position, with her left arm extending down the length of her body and her right arm outstretched at right angles to her torso. Her right hand and forearm were partially hidden among the undergrowth. The rest of Pearl's clothing, her black sweater, blouse, underskirt and bra, were unceremoniously piled on top of the lower part of her body. The soles of her feet were showing through the stockings as if they had been worn through or torn off. Bradley was surprised that he could not see any visible wounds to the body as it lay face down but, given the amount of blood discovered in Weir's field, he was in no doubt at all that when it was time to turn her over, it would be a different story.

Nothing ever moves quickly at a crime scene. Even some 40 years ago a methodical, step-by-step approach had to be closely adhered to in order to secure best evidence. Maps had to be prepared, samples recovered from the area surrounding the deceased, and photographs taken of the body both in situ and when it was eventually moved and taken to the mortuary for examination and postmortem. There was always a risk of transfer and cross-contamination, and all those who did not need to be anywhere near the inner cordon of the scene were simply kept away.

Sergeant John Berry, from the mapping section at police headquarters, attended at around 5pm, and after being shown the location of the body, set about drawing up detailed maps of the relevant areas. Sergeant Norman McKeown, an RUC photographer, took 11 photographs at the crime scene, some of the deceased and the others of various exhibits as they had been identified to him.

Eventually Dr Morgan, the forensic officer on call at the time, arrived from the Verner Street laboratories in Belfast. He examined Pearl's body as it lay face down, and only when he was ready did he ask for assistance in turning the body over.

Bradley could now see exactly where the majority of Pearl's injuries were. Much of her face was bloodstained and her lips were swollen and covered with congealed blood. It appeared that her nose had probably been broken as the bridge showed bruising which spread to both eyes. There was obvious bruising and discolouration around her throat, and in particular close to her windpipe. But it was the puncture wounds to her body which most clearly demonstrated the ferocity of the attack. She had been stabbed several times, at least twice in and around her breasts.

It was a sight which all who witnessed it would never forget. This innocent young woman lying discarded in the hedge, dumped unceremoniously by some crazed killer after she had been brutally beaten and stabbed. It must have crossed their minds that there was a sexual element to the crime, but nothing could be determined until the postmortem had been carried out. Before that there was the very painful but necessary job of formal identification of the deceased.

The anguish and distress experienced by all the Gamble family that day must have been unbearable. The sister who had gone to work at the Damolly Mill had been sent for, and she had returned to the house during the latter part of the morning to comfort her parents and siblings. But the task of identifying Pearl's body was beyond any of them at the time. It was left to her uncle, William Gamble, to attend Newry Police Station later that day to identify his niece. He had last spoken with her before Christmas, just a few weeks earlier, and the battered and bruised body that now lay before him was a sight he had never imagined he would see.

In many cases of murder, where the family have been informed of the event and have not themselves witnessed the demise of their loved one, there is often a sense of doubt and disbelief. They cling to the hope that some kind of a monumental mistake has been made, and sit expectantly waiting for that person to return home. When William Gamble came to the door of the little house at Damolly that evening, there was no doubt. He didn't need to say anything: the look on his face spoke volumes.

CHAPTER TWO
PRIME SUSPECT

The importance of the first 48 hours in any investigation, particularly one involving a brutal murder such as Pearl Gamble's, would not have been lost on the small team of detectives, some of whom had been drafted in from Belfast to assist in the initial follow-up. It was imperative that a detailed picture of Pearl's movements the previous evening be established, and any identifiable witnesses interviewed as soon as was practicable. Those who had attended the dance, in particularly the males, would have to be spoken to and either ruled in or out as potential suspects. Such was the ferocity of the attack on Pearl, it seemed very unlikely that the murderer was not a male.

The pace at which the investigation moved is clear from

the role that Head Constable O'Hara outlined in his deposition as presented to the Spring Assizes in April of that year. From the moment he attended Pearl's family home at 9.45 on the morning of her reported disappearance, he would remain actively involved in the events of those hours, and would not return home again until the early hours of the next day, after police had identified their prime suspect. Not only did he attend the scene, seize vital evidence and take part in the initial search, he was also present during the identification process with William Gamble, and at 10pm that same day assisted other detectives as they spoke with several people who had been requested to attend in order to help with the inquiry. No one could fault O'Hara in his determination to push matters forward with the utmost urgency. It seems that neither he nor any of the others involved in the investigation would rest before they were satisfied that they had done everything physically possible to move one step closer towards finding Pearl's killer.

Should the same events have occurred 40 years later, however, O'Hara's valiant efforts and dedication to duty may have been viewed in an altogether different light, with his actions possibly compromising any potential court case against an accused. Murder cases in recent times have been won and lost on forensic evidence alone, as advances in forensic science have enabled investigators to place suspects at crime scenes through

DNA or fibre transfers, for example, with the court fully accepting the science of this type of forensics as wholly evidential. In a modern policing context the role of an investigating officer in a case similar to this, and in particular an officer who had taken possession of vital evidence from the crime scene and helped to recover the body, would have ended there, at least for the day, to avoid his coming into contact with other evidence or possible suspects. If he had then chosen to continue in a hands-on capacity, only to have come directly into contact with a prime suspect, as O'Hara had, serious questions would have been asked.

Police officers today are continually schooled in the importance of scene preservation and the possibilities of transference of evidence, with the emphasis being on minute residual evidence, often referred to as a trace. Those who attend at the scene of a serious assault or worse have to consider that they may have come into contact with some trace evidence. It is considered bad practice for any of those officers then to become involved in the follow-up arrest of potential suspects directly after having attended the scene, unless, of course, this is unavoidable. The mantra here is 'every contact leaves a trace', adopted from a quote by the well-known criminologist Edmond Locard. Any cross-contamination could prove to be the key element in challenging a prosecution case.

Of the many people who attended the station that evening to account for their movements the previous night, there was one who stood out. This was a 26-year-old, part-time shoe mender and agricultural labourer named Robert McGladdery. He had been visited earlier that day at his home at 4 Damolly Terrace in Newry by Detective Sergeant Robert Knox, Detective Sergeant George Gibson and Head Constable Thomas McComish.

Several doors had been knocked on that afternoon, in particular those of the homes of the people known to have been at the dance, and these young men and women were asked the same questions by police officers. Did they remember seeing Pearl leave the dance? And did they know how she had got home? More importantly, they were all asked to produce the clothes they had worn the night before. The police officers had arrived at McGladdery's door at 4.45 that afternoon to make the same routine enquiries, a full 15 minutes before Pearl's body was uncovered during the search. Even though they all knew deep down that they were investigating a murder, they made it plain to McGladdery and his mother that they still considered Pearl to be missing but that they were not ruling out foul play.

Neither DS Knox nor DS Gibson had to introduce himself to the only man of the house. Robert McGladdery had been in trouble with the police before, and had, since the age of 11, been caught up in various criminal activities. Of those who knew McGladdery and his family, many believed that the early death of his father in 1950 and the consequent lack of a dominant male role model in his life was the catalyst which drove him towards a career in crime.

Born on 10 October 1935 at Derrybeg, Bessbrook, Robert Andrew McGladdery attended Windsor Hill Primary School and then Rockvale Public Elementary School until the age of 14. He was described as being of average intelligence, capable enough, but his school career was blighted by unofficial absences. He went on to work for a year as a labourer at the Blackstaff Spinning Mill in Newry, the rest of his employment being either across the water in England, in factories such as KMP metal products in Lancashire and Valor stove company in Birmingham, or of a casual nature back in his home town. Many of his employers would have described him as a good worker, steady and reliable, but his criminal antics were always causing him to move from one area to another.

Burglary and theft were the first offences Robert committed and which brought him to the notice of the courts at the tender age of 11. On that occasion, on 23 May 1946 at Newry Petty Sessions, he was given credit for a swift guilty plea and after an adjournment was ordered to pay nine shillings in compensation and a further four shillings in costs. Of course it was Robert's parents who would have to foot the bill and not him, as he was still at school. And it wasn't long before he became a major liability to them, for in July 1947, after another charge of burglary and theft, or larceny as it was more commonly known then, he was discharged into his mother's care on a sum of £5 bail for three years.

As he reached manhood Robert celebrated his first 18 years on this earth with an appearance at the Winter Assizes at Downpatrick, where he was convicted of two counts of robbery, commercial burglary and theft, and sentenced to three years' detention in borstal, as rehabilitation centres for young offenders were then generically known. Of this three-year term Robert would be required to serve only one-and-a-half years, as the rule of 50 per cent remission still applied to borstal. It was here, in Malone Training School, that Robert first learned his trade as a shoe mender, one to which he would return on various occasions throughout his life. From his subsequent criminal record it is clear that on being released Robert had made a decision to relocate to England. This was possibly in order to make a fresh start, but it is more likely that he was conscious that he had already made too much of a name for himself among the local police and needed to find new hunting grounds. His own particular brand of violent crime had been a cause of concern for the local constabulary, as it seemed that he acted instinctively without ever giving real thought to or planning what he was doing. He had even attempted to rob the very place he was working in, Blackstaff Spinning Mill, by holding up the night watchman and trying to force the strongroom door. If the very unpredictable nature of his crimes was worrying, his use of weapons was even more so. As a result his decision to take himself off to work on the mainland was welcomed by all at Newry Police Station.

But even with an opportunity to turn his life around, Robert ended up back in borstal for two counts of theft in late 1954, only this time his sentence was meted out by a court in West Sussex. It was then an ever-downward spiral as the very next year, in Devon, he was sentenced to three years in an adult prison for a number of commercial burglaries and for taking and driving away a motor vehicle. All in all, at the same court he had a further 21 cases of burglary taken into account. He had obviously been prolific in his offending, and there were now indications that alcohol had featured heavily in each instance. But it was his conviction at Norwich City Assizes in 1957 for wounding that offered an insight into how Robert McGladdery was developing a taste for violence.

After finishing his prison term on the mainland, McGladdery returned to Newry, dragging his reputation with him, only to end up being convicted of wounding with intent at Newry quarterly sessions in 1959. He may have counted himself lucky that he did not receive a heavier sentence for this crime, in which he had stabbed James Joseph McDonald four times in the back and the legs without provocation. The maximum sentence the court could apply for this offence at the time was life imprisonment, but there are few judges, even today, who will invoke the full penalty allowed by the law. If a stiffer sentence had been imposed, history may have taken a different turn, but I suspect that each term of incarceration McGladdery experienced was feeding his psychosis.

Given his extensive criminal record, those police who knew him, in particular those who had dealt with him in his late youth, would have been under no illusion that he was capable of almost anything, including a crime of extreme violence.

When the three police officers entered McGladdery's home, DS Gibson took the lead in the questioning and it wasn't long before the young man admitted that he had seen Pearl at the dance and had danced with her. But it was McGladdery's mother who offered the next bits of information to the police, information which would later prove difficult for either her or her son to explain. She stated that she had returned home from her work at the Damolly Mill at around 11.20 that morning and spoken to her son, who, she said, was still in bed. She had told Robert what had happened and he had admitted to her that he had seen Pearl and had danced with her, but that he had watched her go home in a car with two other boys.

McGladdery didn't offer up any information other than that he himself had walked home from the Orange Hall without seeing a soul on his journey. With his next breath he said, 'I wish I could get my hands on the boy that done this. You wouldn't have to deal with him.'

When asked about what he had worn the previous evening, he gestured to the dark-blue suit he now had on over a dark-blue shirt, and said that those were the clothes in question. He was also wearing a pair of dark-blue suede shoes, which he said he had likewise worn the previous evening. His clothes were examined by DS Gibson for any signs of blood or obvious marks, but there were none. McGladdery had described the suit as the only one he owned. When asked what overcoat he had worn, he pointed to a full-length brown herringbone one which was hanging from the kitchen door. He stated that this was the only overcoat he owned. Before he was asked about a tie, he lifted one which was draped over a nearby chair and gave it to the police.

A mother's love is immeasurable. The instinct to protect her offspring sees no boundaries. As the three sombre officers stood in her kitchen, probing her son about his activities the previous night, I can fully understand how Agnes McGladdery would have said anything to divert their attentions away from him, in an attempt to keep him out of harm's way. We know that he was no angel and had a history of being on the wrong side of the law, but what mother could believe that her own flesh and blood could be capable of murder? So she did not hesitate when she spoke up on her son's behalf and told Gibson, 'That's the only suit he has.'

There were lots of loose ends accompanying McGladdery's versions of events, and without hesitation he agreed to go with them to the station to make a statement. He was not under arrest and he had not been cautioned for any offence. As far as he was concerned, he was accompanying them of his own free will, to assist them with their investigation. He was cocky and confident, saying to Gibson, 'You know me, Sergeant, I wouldn't do a thing like that. I'll give you all the help I can to get the boy who done this.'

It was only a short time later, at 5.25pm, that DS Knox recorded a statement from Robert McGladdery at Newry Police Station. McGladdery was not the prime suspect at this point, although all three officers who had called on him could not suppress their gut instinct that there was something just not right about his story. Also, he had scratch marks just under his right eye which they had all seen and commented on among themselves. Surely it wasn't going to be this easy.

The amount of blood which would have been present on the clothes of the killer would have been impossible to conceal. But this young man's clothes were as clean as a whistle, with not a trace of blood, or anything else for that matter.

Robert McGladdery recounted to the police his movements on 27 January 1961, the day of the dance. He stated that he left home that day around 1.30 in the afternoon and walked into Newry to sign on the dole. After getting his money from the dole he went into Holywood's public house, where he met up with William Copeland. After a few drinks and a few games of darts, he stated, both he and Copeland walked to the house in Talbot Street where Copeland lived and had tea. Afterwards they walked out to McGladdery's house, where McGladdery had a wash, and then they walked straight back down to Holywood's for more drink. From there they walked to another pub, Magee's, and stayed there from about 8.30 until 10. Next came a visit to St Catherine's Club and yet another drink, before they moved on to the Legion Club, where they remained until 11.30. McGladdery was vague about the time they arrived at the dance at the Orange Hall, but it is clear that between 12.30 and 1am he danced twice with Pearl Gamble.

It is interesting that McGladdery did not attempt to distance himself from the contact he had with Pearl on that night. He would have known that there were several witnesses who could put both of them together on the dance floor, and he wanted to appear credible, in this at least. However, he was emphatic that although he knew Pearl, he did not know much about her. He even stated that they did not have much conversation when they were dancing, yet he clearly said that he was 'related' to her. It sounds as though he may have been thinking on his feet, attempting to turn suspicion away by suggesting a family tie or bond.

McGladdery went on to say that he left the dance at about 1.50am, waiting at the door briefly for a girl he named as Joanie Donaghue, whom he said he had agreed to walk home to Canal Street. When she did not turn up, he said, he walked home via the Belfast Road, arriving at around 2.30am. He further stated that he did not see anyone on the road home, other than a few cars.

What he did clearly say is that he did not know how Pearl Gamble had got home and that he had no idea if she was still in the dancehall when he had left. He also denied ever telling his mother that he had seen Pearl get into a car with two boys.

In relation to his clothing of the previous night, he again confirmed that the same dark-blue suit and dark-blue shirt he then wore were the same clothes he had worn at the dance. The herringbone overcoat and the tie were also referred to as being the same from the night before. McGladdery then signed the statement, and when he had done so, Knox asked him if he knew where Pearl Gamble lived. He replied that he did not, other than somewhere in the country.

Like it or lump it, Robert McGladdery had now committed himself to a story which contained some degree of truth about his movements during the earlier part of the previous day but fell well short of anything close to the actual events of later that evening. He was about to be challenged almost immediately on certain aspects of that story, and again would have to think quickly and provide credible answers.

He must have forgotten his own notoriety in the town where he lived. Here was a young man already known to the police and many other members of the community as a violent and unpredictable individual with a somewhat chequered past. It was impossible for him to have faded into the background at the dance and not have been noticed. He was flamboyant and an extrovert, anything but a shrinking violet. In fact he had spoken to a young constable on duty who had looked in at the hall around the same time that he himself had arrived there.

Constable David Adams was coming to the end of his shift that Friday night when he went to the Orange Hall and stood just inside the inner door. He was already aware who McGladdery was, and recognised Will Copeland as a local. As Adams stood there, he observed

McGladdery entering the hall wearing what he described as a 'fawn coloured three-quarter-length "shortie" coat'.

McGladdery and Copeland stood for a while before heading towards the cloakroom. On their return McGladdery stopped right in front of Adams. The suit which the officer observed him wearing was light-blue or grey, in an Italian styling, with a faint white line in the material. Adams had actually seen McGladdery wearing the fawn 'shortie' coat not long before, at a dance in late January that year at St Colman's Hall. There could be no mistake.

On seeing McGladdery at the police station, located in Newry barracks, and being aware of his answers in relation to what he had been wearing the previous night, Constable Adams could hardly contain himself. When Knox had finished recording McGladdery's statement and was leaving the room, Adams pulled the Detective Sergeant aside and told him what he knew. He was emphatic that the suit was totally different from the one he had seen McGladdery wearing at the dance. He also told Knox that he had not seen any marks on McGladdery's face the previous evening, yet he appeared to have fresh scratch marks below his right eye. There was now a buzz about the station. The officers had reasonable suspicion to believe that McGladdery was in some way involved in Pearl's murder. Knox made a decision to again put the question about the clothing to the young man who was now sitting in the next room.

When McGladdery again denied he had worn a different suit to the dance, Knox double-checked with Constable Adams as to the best description of the overcoat and suit he had witnessed him wearing. Only then did he deem it appropriate to caution McGladdery and put it to him about the light-blue or grey suit and the fawn 'shortie' overcoat.

The answers that Robert McGladdery now gave to Knox were bizarre. He had only just put his signature to a statement in which he denied wearing any clothing other than that which he now had on, but he almost immediately admitted that he had 'possibly' worn the items Knox had described to him. When he was then asked as to where those clothes were, he began to concoct an explanation so elaborate it was almost laughable. He painted a picture of himself to Knox as some kind of shady underworld figure involved with criminal activity across the country and beyond. Knox had simply asked where the clothes were, and McGladdery had answered, 'Supposing they are out of a big job across the water, you fellows would follow them up, and I would get five to seven years in Dartmoor.'

Knox tried to keep him on track, stressing that he was well and truly focused only on Pearl's murder, and that it would be in McGladdery's interest to produce the items. But McGladdery kept up the Walter Mitty pretence, saying, 'I cannot produce the suit. If you give me 48 hours I can produce the shortie coat, but not the suit.' If the coat could be produced, Knox asked, then why not the suit?

'It just can't be got, but the shortie coat can,' McGladdery replied.

Not one of the investigation team was in any way taken in by his story. There was no mistaking it: they now had their prime suspect. But, from what they could tell, he had already either hidden or disposed of the clothing, and their only concern was how quickly they could organise a search of his home to secure the vital evidence. While he was in custody, they also intended to have him medically examined, and would take intimate samples, such as pubic hair, for forensic comparison. So far, all they were basing their suspicions on were the blatant lies he had told in making his statement and the unlikely excuse he had offered as an explanation for those lies. What they needed was clear evidence, and more witness information, in order to weaken the other elements of the story which he was rigidly sticking to.

Later that evening, at 7.45, McGladdery agreed to be examined by Dr Paddy Ward, a GP from Bessbrook, who was acting on behalf of the police during their investigation. Again, had this case been under investigation today, the possibility of cross-contamination could have been an issue here, as Dr Ward had actually attended the scene to pronounce the victim's life extinct and observe body temperature and advancement of rigor mortis. That had been at 6.15pm, just an hour and a half before he was introduced to the suspect.

Dr Ward's findings in relation to McGladdery were that he was a fit and muscular young man, but that he had some marks on his person, noticeably a scratch about three-quarters of an inch long just below his right eye, and a further mark, about half an inch long, below that. When he had asked McGladdery how he had sustained the marks, he had replied that while training with a set of chest expanders, trapping one handle under his foot and pulling upwards with his right hand, they had slipped and caught him on the cheek. Dr Ward was anything but convinced by his answer. There were also cuts and abrasions on the suspect's right hand, one of them, close to the wrist, of a distinctive circular shape. The cuts themselves were fairly deep, and McGladdery suggested that they were part and parcel of his job as a shoe mender, working with the tools of his trade, in particular pincers and a knife. All of the injuries appeared fresh to the doctor, although McGladdery said he had no idea when he had received them.

What Dr Ward found of particular interest was the fact that the young man's hair and skin had appeared to be scrupulously clean, suggesting he had bathed a short time before the examination. His skin was almost red raw, consistent with having been scrubbed or towelled extremely roughly. Samples of head and pubic hair were taken with consent, and scrapings from under his fingernails taken and placed in test tubes and given identifying evidential markings. Throughout this whole process McGladdery showed no fear or nervousness, and was described by Dr Ward as cooperative and respectful.

It must have been quite disconcerting for the detectives dealing directly with McGladdery as he remained cool under the pressure of their continual questioning. More than once they must have thought that they were dealing with a competent and calculating adversary, someone clearly forensically aware and confident that he had done enough to distance himself from anything other than circumstantial evidence.

But the crime itself, and in particular the crime scene, showed all the signs of rage and extreme violence. No attempt had been made by the killer to clean up at the scene either during or after the events. A trail from the first assault to the eventual hiding place of the body had been fairly easy to follow. There had been no shallow grave, and no real effort made to conceal the remains. Was the man they had in custody capable of losing his control to such a degree that he would have left such obvious signs of murder and mayhem? Or was he in some way disturbed, a sociopath incapable of remorse or regret, but with an acute instinct for self-preservation? Whatever theories they had, they knew that the hardest part of the investigation was yet to come.

Shortly after McGladdery returned to the interview room he was told that DS Knox and DS Gibson would be calling in at his house to recover some items. Again he did not seem at all worried by the further developments. The two detectives arrived at the little house he shared with his mother at 11pm that night, and there Knox took possession of two handkerchiefs and a face cloth from a wash basin set out in the back yard. Gibson removed the sheet and blanket from McGladdery's bed, along with a white shirt with black dots. He made an observation at the time that no pillowcase was present on the top pillow but there was one on the pillow below.

Time was ticking by and before long the team would be faced with the prospect of either charging the suspect and detaining him in order to bring him before the first available court, or releasing him pending further enquiries. As yet, they had no solid evidence, and without the clothes he had worn the previous night, or for that matter any hint as to the type of murder weapon or weapons they were looking for, they were somewhat backed into a corner.

For his part, McGladdery was continuing with his ridiculous charade. Head Constable McComish had a further conversation with the suspect after cautioning him, and asked again why he would not produce his clothing. McGladdery's reply was the same as before, 'There is something else there I don't want you to get. This morning when I heard the girl was missing and bloodstained clothing found, I knew the first person the police would look for would be Robert, and if I had a stolen suit and coat I would probably get three or five years, but I am not saying I had a suit or coat.'

Again McGladdery asked for time in order to produce the clothes, now suggesting he could do so within 36 hours. Intrigued as to why he needed as much time as a day-and-a-half, McComish asked him why so long. To this McGladdery replied that he knew that if he was released the police would be tailing him and he would be trying to shake them off, adding that he would even agree to call McComish before midday the next day to tell him where the items were.

Whatever game McGladdery thought he was playing, he must have believed that he was winning when, later that night, he was released and allowed to return home. It is not clear who made the decision to free him, but as County Inspector Ferris of the CID was the senior investigating officer, the last word would have fallen to him. Maybe it was thought that McGladdery would lead them to the hidden evidence, or perhaps he would make a run for it. Whatever the suspect's intentions, he had been right in thinking that he would be under police surveillance. They couldn't afford to have this man disappear. At that point there were no other likely suspects. Everyone felt in their guts that McGladdery was their man, and there were no doubts.

The whole team were now totally focused on piecing together the parts of the puzzle which would hopefully lead to the man's arrest and charge. That determination was to grow even stronger when Head Constable O'Hara returned from Belfast the next afternoon with the results of the postmortem performed on Pearl Gamble's remains.

It is a blessing for us all that, should we be the subject of a postmortem examination, we will be blissfully unaware of the whole ordeal. On the other hand, having had to attend more than a few in my time as a serving police officer, I have always found it an unsettling experience.

Unfortunately, these days, when a sudden death is reported and it can be determined that the deceased had not attended their doctor in over 28 days, the coroner will almost always instruct that a postmortem be carried out to determine the cause of death. It would be oh-so-simple were the person's GP aware of an ongoing heart condition or similar possible contributory illness and could issue a death certificate and spare the grieving family more heartache. In my own experience this is seldom the case.

Nor are there any easy ways for a pathologist to make the process more palatable. The body of the deceased holds the many answers sought in relation to cause of death and the methodology of the killer. A postmortem is an extremely invasive procedure, and not for the weak-stomached or easily shocked.

As if she had not been through enough, Pearl's body had lain on an examination table, naked, save for the remnants of her torn stockings and the remainder of her suspender belt. Her jewellery had been removed and itemised, and her injuries were then measured and recorded by state pathologist Dr Marshall in an attempt to arrive at a definitive cause of death.

Pearl was five feet four inches in height and weighed about eight stone, an average build for a girl of her age. The external examination noted the mud and debris from the undergrowth covering various parts of her body, mixed in some places with smatterings of blood. Cuts and bruises covered her face and forehead, and it was immediately clear that she had sustained at least one violent blow to the face which had broken her nose. Blood trailed from both her nostrils, and she had bruised and puffy upper and lower lips.

There were multiple lacerations around her temples and both ears, some of which were invasive into the muscle beneath. Significantly, there was reddish bruising around her neck, in the area of the thyroid cartilage, and a bluish discolouration stretching around the neck almost to the nape. More clearly defined were the puncture or stab wounds on her chest, all of which appeared deep.

The terminology used by the pathologist during a postmortem has become more familiar as a result of the many crime series on television involving police forensics, such as *CSI* and *Law and Order*. Back in 1962, however, even Head Constable O'Hara would have had trouble interpreting Dr Marshall's findings, and had to wait until after the postmortem to have these simplified. Of course a typed report would have to be made, and it would become the body of the pathologist's statement, but right then, O'Hara needed to know the rudimentary details: the 'hows' and 'with whats'. That is what he needed in order to move things forward quickly, and he pressed the pathologist for a synopsis.

What Dr Marshall relayed to O'Hara, which was later to be repeated in his report and statement, effectively outlined Pearl's last few minutes on earth as he could interpret from her injuries. She had sustained a broken nose and bruising around the cheeks and lips from what he described as 'blows of considerable severity'. These, he surmised, would have stunned the victim and caused profuse blood flow, some of which she may have swallowed, as there had been blood in the upper part of her small intestine. The pathologist also believed that this incident may have started in the lane, and certainly would have accounted for the bloodstained clothing. The interval between this point and the possible time of death would have been 15–30 minutes.

Pearl must have been fighting for her life, desperate to get away from a maniac who had clearly lost all control. Just yards from the safety of her home, where her family lay in bed oblivious to the horror, she edged away from him into the field.

According to Dr Marshall, the killer's attack was relentless, and he pursued his victim into the field and began stabbing her in the right-hand side of her neck and head. The resulting five puncture marks bore a similar pattern to the three further stab wounds on the victim's left chest, in that they looked as though they could have been caused by the tang of a file, the projection which takes the handle. The wounds to her neck and head may have been caused by the killer attacking her from behind, using his right hand to administer the blows, and this too would be consistent with the findings in relation to the frontal chest wounds.

Pearl must have been still struggling to get away when the killer caught up with her, turned her around and began stabbing her in the chest. The first two stab wounds were found to be about two inches in depth and had not done any great damage, but the third wound had entered just above the left nipple and had punctured the heart, causing blood to escape into the surrounding sac. The track of this wound was through the bony part of the fourth rib, and Dr Marshall concluded that a great deal of force must have been used for the instrument to have penetrated her in this way. Again the pattern of each wound was identical, and he again suggested they may have been caused by the tang of some sort of file.

Because of the amount of blood found in the sac during the postmortem, Dr Marshall was confident that the blows had not killed her. He believed that she could have survived another 15 minutes or so, had the attack stopped there. But we know it did not, as the ligature marks on Pearl's neck, along with 'pinpoint' haemorrhages in the skin and lining of the eyelids, larynx, pharynx and the lungs, were telltale signs of death by asphyxia.

In short, Pearl had been badly beaten and stabbed, and as her life blood began to drain away, and all the fight had gone from her, she had then been strangled. A small consolation for her family was the fact that she had not been sexually assaulted in any way.

With regard to the murder weapon, Dr Marshall was clear that the unique star pattern left around the opening of the wounds was consistent with the square or rectangular shoulders of a file. In the coming weeks he would acquire and test several files in an attempt to reproduce the wounds found on the deceased, and to identify the exact type of file used in the attack.

As O'Hara was imparting this news to the rest of the team, the investigation was gathering momentum. The suspect had been released, but he was under constant surveillance, and his movements the previous night were gradually being pieced together. They still needed to establish all three key points which would together identify McGladdery, and him only, as the prime suspect: means, motive and opportunity.

CHAPTER THREE

THE LAST DANCE

As Robert McGladdery's statement relied heavily on what he said about his movements after the dance, and on the fact that he had denied either owning or wearing a fawn coat or a grey/blue suit, the police had a starting point from which to begin breaking down the elements of his story.

The other witnesses at the dance, particularly those who had stayed until the end, could prove vital in providing evidence that might contradict the suspect's statement. But the investigation team had to be selective in sorting the wheat from the chaff, as there had been around two hundred people at the dance that evening and many of these would provide them with little information but still cost them dearly in terms of time.

Good old-fashioned detective work would be the key to the case. Every snippet of information could provide another small piece of the jigsaw and bring them one step closer to knowing just what had happened to Pearl.

What was becoming apparent, however, was that almost from the moment they had returned with Robert McGladdery to the station, everyone in the town seemed to know that the RUC were not looking any further for their prime suspect. Just how information as sensitive as this had been leaked to the general public is not known, but it was an awkward position for the police to be in. In fairness, they could not point the finger directly at Robert until enough evidence had been gathered and assessed. Despite this restraint, they could not stop any witnesses from forming their own opinions as to his guilt, even though it could potentially taint their recollections of the events. Even the local newspapers concentrated on the fact that the police were searching high and low for clothing worn by the killer, clothing which officers knew had been discarded. If they knew it had been got rid of, then they likely had a suspect.

The first and possibly the most important statements were those taken from the four people who had been the last, other than the killer, to see Pearl alive. Evelyn Gamble, Rae Boyd, Billy Morton and Derek Shanks all travelled back from the dance with Pearl in a car driven by Shanks. Evelyn had spent the latter part of the dance with Billy Morton, and as any good friend would do, made sure that Pearl was not left out of the car for the lift home. She was sure that she had not told Pearl about the arrangement for a lift home until around 1.50, just ten minutes before the dance ended. As she and the other three waited in the car on the Belfast Road, they saw Pearl and a young man called Joe Clydesdale in Church Avenue, and when they drove around beside the couple, Pearl said good night and joined Evelyn in the back seat. Evelyn remembered arriving close to Pearl's house and letting her out at around 2.30.

The newspapers reported at the time that just before they had reached the Upper Damolly crossroads, Pearl had said to all in the car, 'Don't bother to come up. Drop me off here and I will be all right.' And to her two girlfriends in particular, 'Don't forget to come up at dinner time tomorrow for a wee bit of craic.'

There is very little variance in the details as seen by Rae Boyd. However, she clearly remembered Robert McGladdery from that night, and the fact that he had danced at least twice with Pearl. She too had danced with him and was even able to recall the light-blue suit and 'something' red around his neck, not committing herself as to whether it was a tie or the colour of his shirt. In a later statement dated 29 January, Rae remembered that during her dance with McGladdery he had made a comment to her, asking something like, 'When did these black stockings come into Newry?'

It was one of many comments he had made to several different women that night, each quip slightly suggestive and flirtatious. From Evelyn's own recollection of the conversation during the journey home in the car after the dance, apparently McGladdery had asked the very same question of Pearl. As Evelyn hadn't really known who McGladdery was, Pearl had to remind her, saying, 'You know, him who has been in gaol a couple of times.'

Still Evelyn wasn't sure, and asked Pearl where he lived, and she thought Pearl had replied either 'beside us' or 'near us'.

Rae Boyd's recollection of arriving at the Upper Damolly crossroads that night was much the same as Evelyn's. She had looked back towards Pearl as they drove away, and saw her dashing across the road towards the lane to her house. She was able to confirm that the time was around 2.30. Both Shanks and Morton confirmed the story, stating that they had set off from Church Avenue for Pearl's house at around 2.15.

Understandably, regrets were voiced when it came to light how and where the murder had taken place. In particular, Derek Shanks found it hard to come to terms with the fact that, had he insisted on driving a few yards further, he may just have saved Pearl's life. That image of Pearl walking away into the pitch-darkness of a winter's night, happy and full of life, would stay with all of them for some time.

It must have been prominent in Rae Boyd's mind too, as she had always worried about Pearl making her way home ever since there had been an incident on the lane near Pearl's front door a few years before. As far as she could recall, one evening, as Pearl was cycling home from the Technical College, a man appeared from nowhere and pulled her off her bike. Her screams apparently alerted her mother and her sister Margaret, and when they came running out of the house to see what was going on, her attacker took off across the fields. No names were ever mentioned as to who it may have been, but afterwards Rae was aware that Pearl was particularly nervous about walking home on the Upper Damolly Road. Whenever the two were out together, Rae would insist on walking her friend as far as the Murphys' house, which was just close enough for Pearl to run the rest of the way to her door. The circumstances of that first incident are startlingly similar to those of the fatal attack on the night of the dance, and this raises the question of whether the same person carried out both.

As the scene of the murder was some distance from the Orange Hall, and McGladdery had said that he had walked home from the dance at around 2am, police now had to establish that he was lying about the time and prove that he could have made it to the Upper Damolly crossroads before Pearl was dropped off. Just how the killer had got there turned out to be simple. He had stolen a bicycle and used it to ride along the same road ahead of her and her friends. The bicycle found just inside Weir's field had belonged to Jack McClenaghan, or rather his brother, and Jack had borrowed it to get to and from the dance that night from his home just off the Tandragee Road. When he arrived at the dance on the Friday night, he had parked the bike against the wall of the telephone exchange next to the Orange Hall. He had left the dance between 1.30 and 1.45am, only to find that it had been stolen.

Even McClenaghan recalled McGladdery being at the dance, and had good reason to remember his shortie coat, as he himself had a similar one, only much lighter in colour.

But had anyone actually seen the person who had taken the bike, or more importantly, had anyone seen McGladdery riding a bicycle on the road that night?

Like many dances of the time, it was difficult for young couples to be in any way intimate with each other, save while dancing close during a slow number. Even then, they would have been wary of the many eyes upon them, and it was more usual to step outside and seek the shelter of a doorway, or if they could, a car, to continue their courting.

When Samuel Moffatt and Maureen Mateer got

together that night, they left the dance at 1.20 and got into a car owned by Tom Sterritt, a friend of Moffatt's. At that time the car was parked on a gravel path beside the hall. Although he was obviously focused on Maureen, Moffatt did see McGladdery come out of the hall and light up a cigarette at around 1.40. Samuel returned his attentions to his young lady, and was only interrupted later when another courting couple, George Dempsey and Marie Hewatson, came out themselves and got into the car along with them. Dempsey clearly thought the car was parked too publicly and so he drove it out on to the Belfast Road and then reversed it in next to the archway beside the wall of the telephone exchange.

But for Dempsey there was still not enough privacy. One couple in a car was all right, but two was stretching it a bit, so he and Marie decided to get out, walking away under the arch and out of sight of Moffatt. It was while the other couple were out of the car that Samuel Moffatt heard a noise in the bushes. Just as soon as he heard the noise, he saw the outline of a man passing close to the car, and heard the distinctive sound of a bicycle being wheeled. Moffatt wasn't sure, but he thought the man may have been wearing a gaberdine coat. Other than McGladdery, Dempsey and Hewatson, the young man had not seen anyone else enter or leave the hall. His female friend Maureen Mateer had also seen the figure wheeling the bicycle, but was unable to give any useful description.

The couple were again interrupted a short time later when Jack McClenaghan returned to get his bicycle for the ride home. After finding it gone, he escorted a young woman as far as Arthur Street, deciding to wait until the next day to report the theft.

Give or take a few minutes, it was clear from eyewitness accounts that the bicycle had been taken at about 1.45am. It was plausible that McGladdery could have been the thief as he had been seen leaving the dancehall around that time. And if he was the thief, there was little doubt that he was the killer as well.

This was a good start for the investigating team, and one which they needed to build upon with more testimony contradicting McGladdery's version of events. Above all, though, they needed to produce good hard evidence. They still needed the clothes.

The police had to adopt a two-tier approach to the case when their prime suspect was released unconditionally the day after the murder. Although he was under constant surveillance, and could lead them at any time to the spot where he had secreted the clothes, they could not afford to sit back and wait. They were confident that they had put the right man in the frame, and now they had to gather every piece of information they could, however small.

In his own words, the suspect had said that he had walked home alone that night along the Belfast Road, arriving at 2.30, when his mother was in bed. Apart from being passed by one or two cars, he had met no one along the way, he said. The police were now keen to speak with anyone who had left the Orange Hall around 2am and had driven or walked along a route similar to the one McGladdery had admitted taking. Was it possible someone had seen him on the road? It certainly had to be considered.

Although the night of the dance had been a typically cold January one, the moon had been full and the air still, just perfect for a romantic walk. Special Constable William Roger Quinn, a member of the RUC Number 12 Platoon Reserve Force in the town, had struck lucky at the dance and had the pleasure of walking Edith Henning home. It was not a long walk, though, as his young date lived just 400 yards up the Belfast Road from the hall, on the same side of the road. When interviewed by the police Quinn was adamant that they had left the dance at around 1.40am, as he had checked his watch shortly before. On their way, the couple would have had to pass the Scriptural Hall, which was where Quinn's platoon was stationed, and he was clear that until they had reached that point on the road he had not seen anyone walking either behind or in front of them. What he did say, though, was that he had a faint recollection of someone riding a bicycle in front of them as they walked towards the Hennings' house, and that it was possibly a man, but other than that, he did not see anyone else.

Miss Henning had obviously caught Quinn's imagination that night, and it would appear that he only had eyes for her, because when she was asked to provide a statement to the police, she clearly remembered a man riding a bicycle up the middle of the road in the direction of Belfast, and cycling by them just as they had passed McCullough's Garage, but before the Scriptural Hall. She was able to add that the bike did not seem to have any lights on and that the rider may have been wearing a grey coat. Significantly, Edith Henning had been wearing a long red coat, which more than one witness was able to remember. As the couple had been approaching the Scriptural Hall, Special Constable Thomas Robinson, who had been on duty that night from midnight, heard their footsteps, and clearly remembered walking up to the gate at the road and seeing the young couple. He also put the time as about 1.40am. He knew Quinn, of course, though not the girl, but he was sure that she had been wearing a red coat.

The young couple arrived at Edith's house at 1.50 and then stood at her door until 2.20. The front door opened on to the pavement, so it would have been easy for them to see anyone pass by. Both were clear that a bike did pass them later on, travelling up the road away from the town, but only Edith was able to say that she had thought the man on the bicycle to be Joe Clydesdale.

If Robert McGladdery had left the dance at 1.50 or after, and had walked home by the route he said he had in his statement, it stood to reason that he would have been seen by Edith Henning or her companion William Quinn. It would have taken him no time at all to cover the 400 yards from the dancehall to her house on his way along the road, and if his timings were correct, he would have been hot on the couple's heels. He had to be lying, either about walking home, or about his route home. Had he in fact been the cyclist that they had seen as they walked hand-in-hand in the moonlight?

Although there were very few doubts as to the fact that McGladdery was their prime suspect, it goes without saying that the police had to keep an open mind in all matters. There must have been a little spark of interest when Joe Clydesdale's name had been mentioned by Edith Henning. After all, it was he who had danced the last dance with Pearl, later walking outside with her and keeping her company as she waited in Church Avenue for her lift home. The only reason for his being regarded as a witness rather than a suspect was that it would have been physically impossible for him to have got ahead of Derek Shanks as he drove his Humber

Hawk towards Pearl's house. Bicycle or no bicycle, it could not have been done.

Yet another person to throw doubt on McGladdery's story was a neighbour of his by the name of William Rees. He too had attended the dance, and besides being able to describe the clothes McGladdery had been wearing that night, he gave an account of his own trip home, during which he did not see anyone. Rees said that he had parked his own bicycle at McCullough's Garage just up the road from the Orange Hall, and had collected it at around 2am. He had then ridden his bike up the Belfast Road and into Damolly, the exact same route which his neighbour would have taken, arriving home at 2.20. Why then had he not passed McGladdery? According to McGladdery's statement to the police, he had not got home until 2.30. Things were beginning to come together for the detectives, with large cracks appearing in their suspect's story as yet more witnesses came forward.

There was one particular young woman who must have considered herself more than lucky when the rumours about McGladdery started circulating the day after the murder. McGladdery himself had referred to her in his statement as 'Joanie Donaghue' but her correct name was Joan Donegan. He had said he thought she lived around Canal Street in the town, and in this he was correct, but that was as much as he knew, or as much information as he had gleaned during the five or six dances he had with her that evening. The man in the 'light-blue Italian cut suit', as Joan had described McGladdery, had grabbed her and spun her around when he first entered the dance. He was brash and forward, she said, and she remembered smelling alcohol on his breath. A short time after coming into the hall, he returned to take her for the first of many dances, and then continued to pester her about whether he could walk her home after the dance had finished. Each time he had asked she had refused, telling him she was going home with her brother. In fact her brother wasn't even at the dance, it was a just a ruse designed to put McGladdery off. Later, towards the end of the dance, she took up with another young man called Teddy Cowan, going out with him to a car about 1.30. She did see McGladdery leave the hall just after another young couple came out, or possibly around the same time, but she was adamant that when she saw him leave the hall he had the fawn shortie overcoat over his arm.

The investigation team were more than happy with Joan Donegan as a witness. She had been in close proximity to the suspect that night on more than one occasion and was clear about the style and colour of his clothes. Much more than that, though, she could provide evidence of his continual pestering to take her home. It seemed that McGladdery had only one thing on his mind that night, and he was not going to take no for an answer.

One young boy, Thomas Halliday, also remembered a conversation he had with McGladdery as he stood with him and Copeland in the dancehall. Out of the blue McGladdery asked him, 'Did anybody harm you or say anything to you?' When Halliday replied no and asked, 'Why?', McGladdery said, 'It wouldn't take them to because I would fix them.' By this he meant that had they made threats he would have dealt with them physically. According to Halliday, McGladdery appeared unsteady on his feet, and in his opinion he was just in the mood for a row.

The team were now confident that McGladdery had left the hall at around 1.40 or 1.45 and taken Jack McClenaghan's bicycle from the telephone exchange. He had then ridden out along the Belfast Road in the direction of the Upper Damolly Road. The next question was, could he have had enough time to make it to the crossroads and lie in wait for his victim?

There were three possible routes the killer could have taken to the scene of the murder after leaving the dancehall on the Belfast Road. Detective Sergeant Gibson decided to time himself both walking and cycling all of these and to enter his findings into evidence. Using a bicycle similar to that found at the scene, he first cycled the routes. The quickest way he found was via

Windsor Avenue, and then the Old Damolly Road, which proved only fractionally quicker than the route via Church Avenue, Rathfriland Road and the Old Damolly Road. Lastly he travelled up the Belfast Road and then into the Upper Damolly Road, and back down towards the crossroads. This last route took DS Gibson just seconds over 20 minutes, with the first two each taking only around 15 minutes. Next he walked all three routes, and again the Belfast Road route was the most indirect of the three, taking 43 minutes as opposed to around 28 minutes for each of the other two.

Gibson was covering all eventualities. No matter what their suspect would say, they now knew that he could also have walked to the murder scene fairly comfortably within the time-frame. But they were still confident that the bicycle was the way the killer had arrived at the scene.

Then Gibson went one step further and added that he knew McGladdery could ride a bicycle, as he himself had witnessed him do so some two years before.

This was going to be the strength of the police case. They were determined to head off any possible lines of defence should they be able to get the suspect into court. A simple fact like the suspect's inability to ride a bicycle could well place doubt in the minds of a jury. All potential boltholes were being covered, and a 'belt and braces' approach was adopted.

Besides the three routes to the Upper Damolly

crossroads taken by Gibson, the route home to McGladdery's house from the dance also had to be covered. If the suspect had taken a bicycle, he would have been able to cover the distance in about eight minutes, and had he walked, it would have been about 15 minutes. So why had it taken him 40 minutes to walk home, as he had told the police?

On Wednesday, 1 February, as officers were again attending McGladdery's home to make further enquiries, and to remove items which they believed could be evidential, Detective Head Constable George Farrelly asked the suspect, after caution again, about his route home the previous Friday night. Surprisingly, McGladdery requested that the policeman accompany him to the Orange Hall, where he said he would gladly point out the road he had taken home that night.

What an opportunity this was for the police. Yet again McGladdery was about to commit himself to a version of events in which he could either trip himself up by contradicting details he had given in his original statement, or further entrench himself in the lies he had told in that account of events.

It is unlikely that at this juncture he had taken any advice from his solicitor, for if he had done so he would have been told in no uncertain terms to avoid unnecessarily assisting the police with their investigation. I believe that McGladdery could not resist playing out this game with the police, thoroughly enjoying the notoriety that the attention was bringing with it, but seriously naive as to the inevitable outcome.

He and Detective Head Constable Farrelly then returned to the Orange Hall, outside which McGladdery began to re-enact his earlier movements for the benefit of his audience. He told Farrelly that he would walk the route at the same pace he had that night, and as he stepped on to the Belfast Road he turned left away from the town and continued along the nearside pavement. The pair walked together for about 30 yards and then McGladdery crossed to the other side of the road, walking a further 50 yards before stopping and looking around. Farrelly was quick to ask him why he had crossed over, as he would only have to re-cross when he eventually arrived at the turning into Damolly village. McGladdery's answer was vague, but he made some reference to McCullough's Garage, saying, 'I was thinking about this garage again. You know what I mean.' His comment suggested that he intended to 'case' the garage for some future burglary or theft, and he had no problem intimating this to Farrelly. Better to be suspected of being a petty criminal than a murderer.

Crucially, McGladdery now turned to the police officer and told him that he remembered turning around at this point and seeing a young couple walking along the other side of the Belfast Road, coming along after him. He even remembered the girl wearing a long red coat, and that they would have been just at the spot where he and Farrelly had just crossed over, about 50 yards away from where they now stood.

McGladdery now concluded that the couple were the only people he had seen on his way home that night. Farrelly was well aware of the content of the suspect's statement made on the previous Saturday, and finally asked him if he had seen anyone at the gates to the Scriptural Hall as he walked further on. McGladdery replied that he had not.

Yet again, he had contradicted his first statement to the police, in which he had said that he had seen no one on the way home. But was this his attempt at being clever? He would have realised by now that other people were coming forward to account for their movements that evening, and if he could in some way tie himself in with having seen the young couple walking up the road, he could throw the police off the scent. What he had achieved instead was to put himself on the road at about 1.40, and most probably on a bicycle, as both William Quinn and Edith Henning were confident that there were no other persons on the road other than the lone cyclist.

This was no exceptional criminal mind at work, but a young man of below average intelligence running rings around himself and getting absolutely nowhere.

He and Farrelly then walked on from that spot for about two miles, until the road to Damolly turned off to the left. They took this and then turned left again into the laneway leading to Damolly Terrace, where McGladdery lived. According to him, the rest of his journey, after seeing the couple, had been unremarkable.

Everyone knew that it had been anything but an unremarkable journey, especially for his victim Pearl Gamble. All the time he was cycling along the Belfast Road towards the Upper Damolly Road and Pearl's house, he must have been playing the forthcoming scenario in his head. He would get there ahead of her, wait until she was dropped off and alone, confront her and then coax her into the field, where he knew she would do exactly what he said. After all, he was Robert McGladdery, the man with just a hint of mystery and danger, irresistible to women. All the girls liked a bad boy, even though they might not admit it, and he was sure he would get what he wanted from Pearl, one way or another.

The police believed they had now established that their suspect had had the *opportunity* in which to have committed the murder, and they were advancing towards identifying the *means* as rapidly as they could. But what of the *motive*? Why had Pearl Gamble been picked out from among the other girls at the dance? Why her?

Often with the murder of a young woman, the motive is of a sexual nature, rape or sexual assault preceding death, with the victim often knowing her attacker. The perpetrator's fear of being identified by the victim often escalates the sexual assault into that of a murder. In this particular case, because the postmortem would confirm that there had been no signs of sexual assault, the police did not consider the motive to have been sexual in nature.

Today there are several arguments to support such reasoning when identifying a motive for a crime similar to Pearl's murder. However, crime behaviour analyst and researcher Antonio Giannone, with a 20-year background in studying crime scenes and case studies, argues that all murders, even those devoid of evidence of sexual assault, should be considered to be sexually motivated. His argument stems from his statement that all murders are premeditated, with murder itself being 'an act of sexual violence'. Theories such as those presented by Giannone are all well and good in today's society, where crime investigation relies heavily on technology and psychology in order to paint a picture of the offender and his motive and modus operandi. But when the team of detectives in Newry back in 1961 searched for a motive for Pearl Gamble's murder, they could not ignore the evidence presented to them by certain witnesses at the dance. For some reason the killer had become fixated on Pearl as she danced the night away with her friends, and the key lay in what they had seen and heard.

Of all the people at the dance who were to come forward and provide witness statements, Gladys Jones, a lieutenant from the Girl Guide group who had helped arrange the evening, appeared to have noticed something peculiar about McGladdery's behaviour with Pearl. She knew both Pearl and her dance partner, and was able to say that she had seen them take to the floor first at around midnight, and then again at 1.15. It was during this second session that she had noticed McGladdery lean his head towards Pearl's, and in her words, 'I thought he was trying to hold her tightly towards him.' Jones went on to describe how at this point Pearl turned her head away from McGladdery, seeming to be uncomfortable.

Others, of course, had also seen the two dancing on at least one occasion that night, Edith Henning and William Copeland among them. Neither had noticed anything particularly bizarre about his behaviour during that dance, however. One other person present that night who was able to add some insight into McGladdery's demeanour was Kenneth Cowan. He had been at the event since early evening as he was a musician playing in the band providing the music. Cowan knew both McGladdery and Pearl by sight at least, and had witnessed them dancing together. It was after their dance, though, that McGladdery had approached the stage and spoken to Cowan, requesting that he play an Elvis number for him. He specifically asked for 'It's Now or Never', and Cowan was both able and willing to oblige. Judging by the reputation McGladdery had in the town, it was unlikely that Cowan would have dared refuse his request. After all, McGladdery was unpredictable, and likely to take issue with him in a physical manner should he not play the song.

As he began playing the first few chords, Cowan remembered, he looked over towards McGladdery who was standing beside the entrance to the hall. It had puzzled him to see McGladdery make no attempt to get up and dance with one of the young women there, but instead stand 'wringing' his hands and looking out towards the dance floor. Cowan estimated this to be around 12.30, which would have been just after Pearl had first danced with McGladdery. As he looked back on what he had witnessed, now knowing what fate lay ahead of Pearl that night, it must have sent a chill down his spine. Was that the point at which the killer had singled out and chosen his victim?

The words of the song which McGladdery requested are certainly haunting. They convey the urgency of a young man's love for a woman whom up until then he has only been able to worship from afar. The song speaks of devotion and love, and the message it sends to its audience appears innocent and pure.

But what exactly did it mean to McGladdery? It is reasonable to assume that in his own mind he had an 'urgency' of a wholly different kind, and one which he intended to placate in whatever way necessary. I also believe he could not differentiate between pure innocent 'love' and his own more base desires. As far as he was concerned, his own 'love' could not wait, and in his desperation he had begun, early on during that evening, to single out the likely candidates to become the recipient of that 'love'. I don't think for one minute that he had any concerns whether the one he chose would be willing or not, or even if that mattered. He was displaying all the signs of a sexual predator, a dangerous opportunist looking to separate a weak victim from the herd.

Had Joan Donegan not told him that she was already going home with her brother, she may have remained the focus of his intention. But she had, not just once but three times. It was clear from his persistence, though, that he was determined. With that avenue explored and proving fruitless, he had moved on to Pearl.

We know that Pearl had taken to the floor for the second time with McGladdery, and from Gladys Jones's recollections of events, that she had in some way been uncomfortable during that dance. There is no way of knowing exactly what he had said or suggested to Pearl as he held her tightly and whispered in her ear, but we can very well imagine. Similarly, we will never know just how she had spurned his advances and whether it was abrupt or said in a manner to spare him embarrassment. Whatever happened, just the fact that this was another outright rejection, another blow to his ego, was seemingly enough to light a fire inside McGladdery, a fire which burned with such ferocity that all semblance of sanity disappeared. The frenzied attack on Pearl was carried out by a virtual madman, and in many ways that is exactly what McGladdery had become. Rejection was the catalyst for the awful events that followed the dance that night. Rejection was something which Robert Andrew McGladdery could not accept.

CHAPTER FOUR

THE MORNING AFTER

The days immediately after the start of the investigation saw some frantic door-knocking in an attempt to identify further witnesses, many of whom would be immediate neighbours of Agnes and Robert McGladdery in the little village of Damolly. The reasoning behind this was again to try to undermine elements of McGladdery's statement to the police, in which he had stated that the first he knew that Pearl was missing was when his mother had returned from the Damolly Mill at 11.30 that morning and had spoken to him as he lay in bed. Agnes McGladdery had sworn to the police that she knew her son had been in bed at 4.30 when she had got up and went down into the kitchen, and again at 5.45 when she was setting off for work. If he were the killer, as they now had no doubt he was, he would have had to have been busy removing any possible evidence that could lead police to his door, and could not have afforded to have lain in bed throughout the night. Even though he had done little to sanitise the scene of the crime at the crossroads, most likely because of the spontaneity of the assault, never mind the enormity of the area within which the evidence lay, in the aftermath of it all his survival instinct would almost certainly have kicked in and forced him to conceal any signs of involvement.

Small rural communities today differ little from those back in 1961. Curtains still twitch and neighbours often know one another's routines just as well as their own. Any deviation from these can upset the kilter of their day and will undoubtedly be noted. What the police believed they would find was some sort of deviation in McGladdery's behaviour, a blip in his routine, and they were counting on him being a creature of habit. They were not disappointed.

For William McGuigan, the sight of Robert McGladdery up and about before ten o'clock any morning was enough to raise an eyebrow. There is very little that gets past the local shopkeeper in a small rural community, and for McGuigan, who rose normally at 7am to open his shop just across the street from 4 Damolly Terrace, at first light there was always something happening that was at least of gossip interest. He knew Robert well enough, including his reluctance to make an early start, even though he had been carrying on a shoe-repairing business from his mother's house for some time. On several occasions McGuigan had accepted shoes from clients on McGladdery's behalf, as they had been unable to raise the young man on calling at his front door. It was no secret that McGladdery was far from dependable and that his 'business' provided barely enough to keep him in beer money. Although the arrangement between the two men was fairly loose, McGuigan was seldom acknowledged by McGladdery, certainly not financially.

So when the police spoke to McGuigan and asked if he had noticed anything peculiar about McGladdery's movements on the morning of Saturday, 28 January, he had no hesitation in speaking up. He had spotted McGladdery at around 7.50 that morning, just a few doors away, carrying a white enamel bucket full of water back from the water pump towards his own house. He had on what McGuigan believed was a red pullover with a blue 'bar' across the chest, and trousers or jeans. It was apparent to the shopkeeper that McGladdery was in a hurry. He remembered passing the time of day with him, but couldn't be sure about the reply he received.

McGuigan was such a compelling witness that Inspector Bradley and his team were left in no doubt that their prime suspect had been up and around early that morning, totally out of sync with his normal routine, and frantically ridding himself of whatever might tie him to Pearl's murder.

The killer couldn't have known just when the body would have been found, and when, if ever, the police would come knocking on his door. But one thing he could be sure of was that he had to stay calm and deal with the loose ends as quickly as possible. His paranoia was clear when just after 8am that morning, a short time after McGuigan had seen him crossing from the pump, Vera Ashe, the manageress of the canteen at the Damolly Mill, had walked past 4 Damolly Terrace and seen McGladdery peering furtively through the curtains into the street. Ashe had just got off the eight o'clock bus from Newry along with a few others, and it may have been the sound of footsteps outside on the pavement which drew McGladdery to the window.

We know from Dr Ward's examination of McGladdery later that evening at Newry Police Station that his skin and scalp appeared to be pinkish red, as if it had been scrubbed clean, or as the pathologist put it, 'towelled roughly'. Everything began to fit. The investigation team were now sure that Robert had waited until his mother had left for work before donning some loose clothes and fetching water in the enamel bucket in order to scrub himself clean of any traces of blood.

A little knowledge is a dangerous thing, and although McGladdery thought he could remove all signs of Pearl's blood from his own body, it was likely that he would not have even considered the residue that his cleansing routine would have left behind. As every new piece of information was sifted from eyewitness accounts and disseminated among the investigation team, the decision as to whether to search and seize items from in and around McGladdery's home was being considered.

With a premeditated sophisticated murder, the killer invariably has the time to make provision for the disposal of vital evidence, and in some cases the body. A plan is hatched and if all its elements come together, then, regardless of the fact that the killer is already under suspicion, without real hard evidence the case remains at best circumstantial.

No such plan was ever hatched in the case of Pearl's murder. No provision was made to either hide the body or dispose of evidence. There had been no premeditation in killing Pearl: it had just happened because matters got out of hand. A simple rejection had sent her killer into a murderous rage and he then had to think on his feet in an attempt to extricate himself from blame. As the days progressed, in his own twisted logic he may have believed that he was parrying every blow that came his way from the investigators, but in reality their net was tightening around him and their case was getting stronger by the hour.

During the early evening of 28 January the police decided to return to McGladdery's house and remove items which they thought could prove evidential should he turn out to be the killer. Detective Sergeant Gibson and his colleague Detective Sergeant Knox arrived at 11pm that night and with Mrs McGladdery's permission removed some items from her son's bedroom and the back yard. It was Gibson who seized the sheet from McGladdery's bed and the blanket next to it, as well as a white shirt with dots printed on it. Knox went into the back yard and found and seized two handkerchiefs and a face cloth from a wash basin. One thing Gibson did notice and deemed important enough to note in his statement was the fact that although there were two pillows on the bed in McGladdery's room, only one had a pillow case on it, and this lay underneath the one which had no cover. His well-honed police instincts told him that there had been a pillow case there previously, but that it was likely that it had been removed earlier that day.

Like all items removed from either a crime scene or the prime suspect's house, these were entered into the chain of evidence, ready to be presented to the court at any forthcoming trial. The first search was always going to be the best opportunity for the police to retrieve any important pieces of clothing or other physical evidence which had been referred to by the suspect or any of the witnesses, or considered to be of importance by the investigation team themselves.

Realistically, though, the search was less than thorough, with the likes of the chest expanders and sludge from the gulley in the yard remaining there until they decided to return a full three days later on 1 February. Even when Head Constable O'Hara and Dr Morgan returned on 30 January to again remove samples from the house, in particular McGladdery's bedroom, they did not consider taking these items.

McGladdery's explanation of the scrapes to his face relied heavily on his assertion that the chest expanders had snapped up from under his foot and caught him under his right eye. So why had the police left them behind? Not only had they left them behind, but as McGladdery had been released from custody late on the evening of 28 January, they had given him ample opportunity to tamper with them in order to lend credence to his story. Also, at this stage, the police suspected that he had been up early that morning and had washed any traces of blood from his body in the back yard of his house. Again, he was afforded a further opportunity to clean up his mess.

It is understandable that the first search did not focus on a potential murder weapon, as it was not known until later the next day, when the postmortem was complete, what type of weapon had been used, or indeed the cause of death. But, assuming that McGladdery was the prime suspect, and there is little doubt that he was even at that stage, in truth it must be considered a mistake that a fingertip search, a more in-depth process, of the house and its confines was not carried out before he was released.

This was a murder inquiry, after all, and one in which the sheer violence visited on the victim would have left numerous traces of blood and other organic material on her attacker. Today, even with lesser crimes, expediency of search after arrest is deemed crucial in securing best evidence of the offence, or of any other criminal acts. If the police arrest a prolific burglar or thief, for instance, and reasonably believe that other items of stolen property or evidence of other offences can be found at their place of residence or anywhere they may have control of, they can be granted an Article 20 search warrant for those premises. The search is then carried out as soon as possible to prevent the potential evidence being concealed, lost, altered, destroyed or disposed of.

We do know that at this stage McGladdery was 'helping' police with their enquiries and was willingly giving his consent for them to search. It could be that his confidence was disarming in some way, throwing them off the scent slightly, so that the first search was at best cursory.

Whatever the reason for the decision to release him before a more thorough search of the premises was carried out, McGladdery was given time to tidy up any loose ends he could think of after his grilling by O'Hara and the others. Thankfully for the investigators, he had not had the presence of mind to take advantage of his freedom, and had left the chest expanders and a set of pincers exactly as they were. Police officers then returned on 1 February and again on 10 February to finish what they had started.

As a murder weapon was never recovered, the question remains as to whether McGladdery had the iron file, or files, in his possession while in police custody late on 28 January, and whether they had been overlooked during the first search that evening.

The fact that Dr Marshall believed the wounds on Pearl's body were likely to have been caused by the tang of a file narrowed the possibilities down for the investigation team. A file would have been common in McGladdery's part-time occupation as a shoe repairer, and it gave them somewhere to start. Could he have returned to the house before waiting for Pearl on the road, and taken the tool from his room? If he had done so, he was premeditating a violent assault. But Agnes McGladdery would certainly have heard him come in and then go away again. However, as her evidence up to that point had been anything but reliable, the police had to make do with conjecture. As well as that, it would have taken McGladdery some valuable minutes to leave the Belfast Road and pick up the file before cycling back on to the main road and then on to the crossroads.

This did not seem a plausible scenario. The question then was whether in fact he had already been in possession of the murder weapon, having it with him at the dance or at least immediately afterwards. But if so, why had he been carrying it around with him at all? There was a simple enough answer to that question, and the police did not have to look far for an answer. According to one person in particular, McGladdery had purchased two files earlier on the day of the dance, and it appears he had simply forgotten to take them out of the pocket of his overcoat.

Undoubtedly one of the most damning statements offered against McGladdery was to come from the single person who knew his every movement in the earlier part of Friday, 27 January, the hours leading up to the dance at the Orange Hall. William James Copeland was able to provide a comprehensive account of both his and McGladdery's whereabouts that afternoon and evening, as it was he who accompanied him at every stage.

For Copeland, a labourer, a Friday afternoon in the pub was about as good as it got, playing a few games of darts with the other clientele and enjoying a quiet pint or two. His job at the Damolly Mill would have brought him in contact with many of the men and women of the town, as the Mill was one of the major employers in the area. But should there have been nobody he knew in the pub, there were always plenty of willing opponents for a game of Round the Clock.

His choice of bar that Friday was Holywood's in Hill Street, a watering hole fairly popular with both young and old. He had been passing the time with a friend by the name of William Smith before Smith decided to move on just after 3pm. It wouldn't be long before Copeland again had company, in the form of Robert McGladdery, or 'Robbie' as he knew him. The two young men had gone to school together and now struck up a conversation almost immediately. In between playing darts the two friends sat drinking at the bar and talking about their plans for the evening. It is ironic that Copeland actually mentioned the dance due to be held at the Orange Hall that night, suggesting it as a place to go, as McGladdery had been considering going to Armagh to another dance. With someone to tag along with, McGladdery quickly changed his mind, and they agreed to stop off for tea at Copeland's house and then to make an evening of it with a few more pints before ending up at the dance.

Copeland's evidence proved to be invaluable.

As Copeland recounted the events to the police, they repeatedly asked him probing questions about McGladdery's appearance, the clothes he was wearing at the time and any marks he may have had on his face or hands. The time-line they were building up from Copeland's information alone was going to be very persuasive to any jury.

As the two young men made their way towards Copeland's house at Talbot Street in the town to grab a quick bite of tea, McGladdery steered them briefly towards Woolworths, saying he needed something for a job he had to do. Both men went up to the hardware counter, where McGladdery began looking at files. Copeland remembered his friend picking up a particular one and saying, 'This is just right for the job.' The file he had chosen, Copeland went on to say, was about five to six inches long, flat on both sides with a pointed end, or tang, for a handle to be put on.

Copeland told the police that he had actually handled the file, one of two identical ones which McGladdery eventually purchased from a young shop assistant by the name of Therese Tierney.

Therese Tierney remembered selling the files to one of the two young gentlemen at around five o'clock that afternoon. But her description of the man she had sold the files to was vague and later she was unable to pick McGladdery out of a line-up. She did remember, however, that when she asked if he had wanted the files wrapped, he had declined, placing them instead in the inside pocket of his 'greyish shortie overcoat'.

It was a very simple piece of information, a minor detail, but in many ways it was vital in placing Robert McGladdery in possession of an item which was believed to be the murder weapon. Regardless of whether the file was ever going to be found, it was very strong circumstantial evidence. A jury would have trouble accepting that it was just coincidence.

The first port of call for the two men after Woolworths was Copeland's house. Both had their tea, after which Copeland changed into the clothes he intended to wear to the dance that evening. At around 6.30 they carried on along the Belfast Road to McGladdery's house, where he would wash and change.

It is likely that as Copeland was recounting his story to the police they were picking up on small, seemingly unimportant details and encouraging him to elaborate on them, teasing the little snippets which were vital to building the bigger picture. It may have been frustrating for him, and he may have considered some of the questions pointless, but he still managed to fill in the more mundane aspects of the events as they unfolded.

In modern police training, recording detailed witness statements and carrying out suspect interviews are taught as particular skills, designed to enhance investigative techniques. In many ways they are quite similar. The questions posed are open, and invite the interviewee to provide information without prompting. They must be encouraged to tell their story, without any details being provided by the police which may suggest outcomes or sway descriptions. It is a difficult technique to adhere to, as we are all prone to reverting to a conversational approach.

If, for instance, the interviewer wished to establish the movements of a suspect on that day, he would ask, 'Can you tell me where you went this afternoon, what you did and who you were with?' These are simple enough questions and the onus is on the suspect to provide a full explanation. However, more often than not, interviewers are too keen to offer information on the suspect's behalf and lead them towards an answer. For example, 'So, did you leave the house and meet up with Smith in the town, and then head to the pub?'

The two answers may be the same, but the second approach is a closed question, and may be construed as leading a suspect, or for that matter a witness, towards a conclusion.

When the detectives involved in the inquiry into Pearl's murder were sitting down with their significant witnesses, it is likely that their interviewing skills had been honed through experience rather than through carefully thought-out lesson plans taught during their basic training. It is said that good police officers are born and not trained, and in some ways I believe that to be the case.

One of the details they were excited about, and on which they further probed Copeland, was where the files had gone to. Had McGladdery at any time taken them from the inside pocket of his shortie overcoat and placed them somewhere in the house. Or, as they now suspected, had he kept them inside his coat pocket? As far as Copeland was concerned, when the two returned to McGladdery's house, his friend had taken off his overcoat and placed it over the bottom of the stairs, over which Copeland then placed his own. At no time had he witnessed the files being removed from the pocket of the coat.

Every little detail was being teased out of Copeland now, with the police building up a three-dimensional picture of the half-hour or so the young men had spent at Damolly Terrace. McGladdery had left his friend for a few moments and had gone into the scullery (kitchen) for a wash. At this point he was stripped to the waist, but still wore the same trousers he had on that afternoon. On returning to the front room where Copeland was, he picked out a red-and-white pinstriped shirt which was ironed and asked Copeland's opinion on ties which were hanging over the back of one of the chairs. It was then that McGladdery took out a set of chest expanders which had been in a cardboard box and showed them to Copeland. He explained to him that he had got them in England and proceeded to show him how to use them. He began by placing one foot through one of the handles and then pulling the other handle up with his arm.

Here was another perfect opportunity for the investigating team to undermine McGladdery's story, specifically his explanation about the marks on his face, which he claimed had been caused by the chest expanders. They couldn't believe their luck. Copeland went on to tell them that McGladdery had completed the exercise at least five or six times and at no time had the device slipped and caught him under the eye. In fact, it was Copeland himself who may have given McGladdery a plausible explanation for the marks, for as his friend was pulling on the chest expanders he had commented that if they were to slip they could 'knock your head off', or words along those lines. This had obviously stuck with McGladdery, who, when put on the spot by detectives at Newry Police Station on the Saturday evening, had likely congratulated himself on some very quick thinking.

As he continued his story Copeland paid particular attention to what he remembered about the clothes McGladdery had chosen to wear that evening. At some point Agnes McGladdery had come home and was chatting with Copeland as her son readied himself for the night ahead. Copeland was particularly clear about the suit that he saw him change into, and the fact that it was light-blue or grey. He also recalled that McGladdery had put on a pair of black leather shoes. These, he was sure, were leather as opposed to suede, as McGladdery had polished them with a brush and then a soft cloth, which Copeland then described as a yellow duster. As Copeland had sat talking with Agnes McGladdery, sharing stories about the Damolly Mill, where both of them worked, McGladdery had been 'sawing' the yellow cloth back and forth over the toes of his shoes with his foot resting on the arm of the settee.

There was also no mistaking the tie that Copeland remembered his friend choosing to wear with his red-and-white pinstriped shirt. Having the choice of several ties, which Copeland recalled hanging over the back of a chair, McGladdery had instead picked up a red one with a blue or black stripe that was lying on the cushions of the settee.

William Copeland was an exceptionally good witness, his recall almost perfect and his cooperation second to none.

After leaving Agnes McGladdery behind at her home, the two young men headed back into town and went straight to Fallone's cafe. There would always have been some activity in this establishment, and both enjoyed a cup of coffee before deciding that on that particular night they were better settling for the pubs. By 8.30 they had already been back to Holywood's and drunk a quick pint, and then they headed on towards Magee's in Merchants Quay. Again, Copeland was happy to play darts, while his partner for the evening propped up the bar. Copeland is never specific about just how many drinks they had that evening, but it was certainly more than a couple. Both had been drinking in the afternoon, and had only stopped for a quick snack at teatime.

Magee's was followed by a stop first at St Catherine's Club and then at the British Legion Club, where they remained until 11.15. It was 11.30 when the two companions arrived at the Orange Hall. Copeland had to give McGladdery five shillings to pay for both of them at the door, and when they stepped inside and looked around they decided to stay and went back to the cloakroom to check in their coats.

For McGladdery, the hunt for his conquest, or as we now know, his victim, had begun in earnest. This was where he believed he would find a woman, willing or not, with whom to quench his base desires. Although the two men stood side by side in the hall during the rest of the evening, parting occasionally to take up with various dance partners, they made small talk only. McGladdery was totally focused on finding someone to take home after the dance had finished.

At the end of the dance Copeland did not see McGladdery again and was left to make his own way home. They had drunk together from mid-afternoon to late evening, and had even stopped for tea at Copeland's house before going on to the dance, but now McGladdery had abandoned his friend in favour of someone or something else. There was not a real bond of friendship between the two; for McGladdery, at least, it was more of a convenient set of circumstances. It seems very likely he had been at a loose end that Friday and had tagged along with Copeland after the suggestion was made about the dance at the Orange Hall.

McGladdery was a parasite and a user, a bully who was hard to refuse, with a reputation as a volatile individual.

CHAPTER FIVE
THE PIED PIPER

I cannot recall a single murder inquiry where, after so quickly identifying their prime suspect, the police have released that person without charge just hours later. Even when the evidence is primarily circumstantial, there are other things to take into consideration, particularly the likelihood of vital forensic evidence being lost or concealed or tampered with by the suspect. By using police powers of entry and search under warrant, that evidence can be secured and seized while the suspect is still held under suspicion of the offence, so that further questioning can take place. Any items recovered would then be shown to the suspect during further interviews and they would be asked to account for them. As the picture of events is built up, the suspect remains in custody, unable to impact upon the situation as it unfolds at either the crime scene or their own place of residence.

During any form of questioning by the police a fairly intelligent suspect can often see the direction of the investigation. It can lead them to adapt their own story in an attempt to distance themselves from any involvement in the crime. If they are released, this could allow them an opportunity to reconsider what forensic evidence they may need to conceal or destroy, and even to approach and interfere with any potential witnesses. The implications of freeing a suspect at such a time can be vast and devastating for an investigation.

Even more worrying is the possibility that the released suspect will flee. Imagine someone has been questioned at length about a brutal murder and can see the net closing tighter around them, but is then presented with the opportunity to make a run from the police. The choice of action is likely to be very easy.

All of these reasons suggest the improbability of Robert McGladdery's being allowed to walk free from Newry Police Station just a few hours after he had been grilled by the murder investigation team. Nevertheless, that is exactly what happened.

The one and only search to take place at McGladdery's house on Saturday, 28 January 1961, while he was still in custody, was conducted by DS

Gibson and DS Knox, and all that was taken as a result of that search were the blanket and sheet from his bed, a white shirt with black dots, two handkerchiefs and a face cloth. Yet this was the best opportunity for them to conduct the most thorough of searches possible, and to seize as many items as they conceivably could from in and around the house. Two full days later, on 30 January, Dr Morgan returned to the house and took several samples from various rooms, and then later still, on 1 and 10 February, police completed their own searches, seizing numerous other items.

The first search at McGladdery's house should have been extensive. If he had been arrested on suspicion of murder at an early stage, and I believe there may have been sufficient grounds to do so, almost every item which may have been relevant to his statement, and other vital trace evidence, would have been recovered earlier. The only important items which would not have been found at the house were the clothes the police knew he had been wearing the night before. I can understand just how important these clothes were, but I believe that had the police thought the matter through they would have realised that keeping hold of McGladdery was much more important, and that a search for the clothes over a considerably wider area might have proved fruitful.

I am not an advocate of 'hindsight policing', unless

there are valuable lessons to be learnt from any errors made in a particular investigation. Each case will be unique, and with it several unforeseen variables will present themselves. But there are strict guidelines laid down in modern policing which are difficult to veer away from, and these exist to steer investigators along a particular path, one which will lead them towards the successful prosecution of a case. There did not appear to be any such aide-memoire in place during the time of the Pearl Gamble murder inquiry. The senior investigating officer therefore would bear the brunt of all criticism of any decisions made in relation to the handling of the suspect or of the case in general, and there were to be many criticisms.

With regard to the evidential items which remained at McGladdery's house and could have been tampered with on his return from the police station that night, it was luck rather than anything else that they were still there when police went back at later dates to search and seize. Whether he was being overconfident, or as I believe, just utterly deluded, McGladdery was convinced he had done enough to throw the police off the scent, in his mind having successfully covered his tracks.

Much more worrying than the potential loss of evidence was the fact that the decision to release the suspect was made at all, considering Newry's close proximity to the border with the Irish Republic. It would not have been difficult at all for him to have crossed into the Republic using one of the several routes which existed only a mile or two from his home. At the time there was no extradition treaty in place between the Republic and Northern Ireland, even though there was an 'agreement' of sorts between mainland Britain and the Irish Government. If he had slipped his police surveillance team he could have been gone for good.

During his questioning on the evening of 28 January, after eventually admitting that he had in fact been wearing a different set of clothes, McGladdery had then concocted his incredible story about the clothes being linked to a theft or robbery on the mainland. He then asked Head Constable McComish for some time, specifically 36 hours, in which to recover the items and hand them in. When asked by McComish why it would take him so long, he replied, 'Well, I know the police will be tailing me, and I'm going to take a gamble that I can shake them off.'

Thankfully McComish did not agree to McGladdery's terms, stating that he himself could not afford to take that particular 'gamble'. But when McGladdery said that, if released, he would allow his home to be searched and would ring McComish the following day and give him the location of the coat at least, a deal of sorts was struck. Even so, he still insisted that it would take him 36 hours to turn up the suit as well. But the coat would be a good start. He was reminded at all times by McComish that he would, of course, be under constant surveillance. McGladdery was brash and defiant replying, 'Well, I'll take a chance, I'll give you a ring between half eleven or [sic] twelve.'

We can only imagine the thoughts running through McGladdery's head as he was taken home to Damolly that night, but I am sure he was smiling all the way there. After all, he had just managed to spin the most ridiculous of stories to get himself released from police custody and back out on the street. But what exactly did he intend to do with his freedom, and for how long could he possibly play this game?

The events of the next 12 days were in some ways to divide the community, and in others to unite it as never before. Doubt and uncertainty spread like a cancer throughout Newry, fed by questions about McGladdery's guilt or innocence. If the police were so certain of his guilt, why did they not just arrest him? Why was he being allowed to roam free about the countryside to do as he pleased? Or, according to another train of thought, had they just pointed the finger at the wrong man altogether?

Sometimes people feel a reluctance to believe the worst about others that they profess to know in some way, because in a sense it undermines their own judgement. It is also common for the authorities, in this case the police, to be lambasted as incompetent or, worse, corrupt, when an investigation is not immediately productive and appears to be slipping away from an early conclusion.

Regardless of speculation and rumour, when County Inspector Walker joined his CID colleague Ferris in heading up the hunt for the killer and locating the missing evidence, the local community showed solidarity in offering their assistance en masse in any search of the fields and surrounding countryside.

This search for evidence which could be linked to the killer began in earnest on 29 January, the day after McGladdery returned home. The RUC crime van, effectively a mobile incident room, had arrived at the crime scene to act as a forward command post to coordinate the search teams. Already the police had rallied some small punts and begun the process of dragging the Clanrye River, just yards from the back of the little row of cottages where McGladdery lived. There was no hiding the facts from the general public, or the press for that matter, and it was soon common knowledge that the objects of the search were a murder weapon and the discarded clothes.

Armed with a brief in relation to the type of murder weapon used, the police now employed five hand-held mine detectors in an attempt to locate any metal objects buried among the thickets and undergrowth. As the weather was set to become colder and the ground harder, coated each morning in a crisp, white frost, their digging and probing was going to be slow and laborious.

As the police combed the fields and lanes around the crime scene that morning, McGladdery was still lying in his bed. His promise to call Head Constable McComish between 11.30 and noon was due to be broken as he seemed intent on having a lazy Sunday morning. He was no doubt considering his next move, and how, if ever, he was going to shake off the two constables who stood watching his terraced house. Whatever he was thinking, he now had to come to terms with the fact that he was under scrutiny no matter what he did from then on. It wasn't house arrest as such, as he would be able to come and go as he pleased, but it was intrusive nonetheless.

Today there are all sorts of pieces of legislation which would restrict the degree with which the police could carry out such an operation, and they all centre around the human rights of the individual in question. Surveillance, which is described as either directed or intrusive, is strictly controlled through the Regulatory Investigative Powers Act, or RIPA for short, and refers in particular to the use of covert methods of obtaining intelligence or gathering evidence to be used against an identified subject or subjects. Unless a RIPA is granted, any surveillance of an individual would not be considered, and if it is carried out without a RIPA being in force, any evidence gained could be considered inadmissible.

Constable Maurice Manson's only concerns on that morning in late January 1961 were whether he could keep himself warm enough and stay alert so as not to miss any movement at the back door of the McGladderys' cottage. He had been directed, if the suspect left the house, to follow him, record all his movements and relay the information to his superior officers. There was also the possibility that McGladdery might make a run for it, and if Constable Manson thought that he was making any such attempt, apprehension of the suspect was paramount.

I am sure Manson must have thought that his time at the house would be uneventful, and the chances of the suspect even coming out would be slim. But, at 2.15pm, Manson observed McGladdery leaving the house by the back door, and walking into a field beside the row of terraced houses. He followed as McGladdery continued into another field before veering left and walking further until he eventually reached the bank of the Clanrye River at a point some two hundred yards to the Belfast side of the Damolly Mill. Manson had followed the suspect at a discreet enough distance, but it had been difficult to maintain any 'follow' without alerting the subject to his presence. At this point he could not be sure that McGladdery had not picked up that he was being tailed. As Manson watched, McGladdery stood for a short time looking all about him, before walking directly into the river and crossing over to the other side. The young constable did not follow him: he would later describe the river as swollen and explain that McGladdery had to cross with his arms extended over his head, the water coming up to his chest at times. From his vantage point he continued watching as the drenched figure walked across another two fields on the other side of the river until he came to Newry Canal, which he then crossed by a footbridge.

Manson's heart must have skipped a beat when he then saw McGladdery enter a partially demolished house which stood beside the far end of the footbridge. Was this the hiding place for the clothes and the murder weapon? Had McGladdery actually believed he had thrown off his police surveillance team so quickly, and returned to get rid of the evidence once and for all? It must have looked more and more promising when McGladdery stayed inside the ruin for about five minutes before eventually resurfacing and walking towards Newry on the towpath. As the suspect continued walking towards the town, Manson breathed a sigh of relief when he saw a car he knew to be driven by Special Constable Crawford racing towards the bedraggled figure.

When Hugh Crawford caught up with McGladdery

he saw that his clothes were soaked from the chest downwards, water dripping from him as he stood talking through the open window of the car. Crawford asked McGladdery to return with him to Newry barracks in order to get him a change of clothes, and he agreed without any fuss.

Even with police resources already stretched to the limit, the route taken by McGladdery on his little jaunt had to be searched, in particular the derelict building he had entered and stayed in for around five minutes. There was no telling whether there had been any real purpose to the journey, or whether it had been designed purely to frustrate and redirect the efforts of the search teams. Nevertheless, it was immediately apparent to the police that their surveillance would have to remain tight for fear of losing the suspect altogether. Judging by the erratic nature of his behaviour, it was a serious risk for him to take, and I am not entirely sure that it was in any way calculated.

The promise of a telephone call to Head Constable McComish had been another stalling tactic and one that McComish must have known was never going to pan out. When he was told about McGladdery's antics in the Clanrye River, he went immediately to Newry Police Station and spoke to him. As McComish entered the small room in the barracks, McGladdery looked up from where he sat drying his clothes by an electric fire.

Asked what he was doing in the river, McGladdery replied, 'I was going to do that job for you, but the police brought me to the barracks.' He added that the only reason he hadn't telephoned at the arranged time to tell McComish where the shortie overcoat was hidden was that he had slept through until after 'dinner'.

Of course, McGladdery had never had any intention of telling McComish where the coat was, and I don't believe that the police were in any way taken in by his ruse. While McGladdery was at the station, a young constable named Gerald Thom, who knew him from around the town and had actually spoken to him at the dance, asked him about the missing clothes and was likewise treated to evasion. McGladdery first kept up the pretence that the clothes he had given police were those he had worn that Friday night. But when Thom reminded him that he had seen him wearing the light-blue suit at the dance, not to mention the fact that he himself had already conceded that he had been wearing it, McGladdery quickly reverted to the story that he was afraid that by handing the real clothes in he would be incriminating himself in another matter for which he could get five or six years in jail.

It was becoming frustrating for all who came in contact with this young man and were subjected to the nonsensical story he had concocted and which he still seemed to expect them to consider plausible. It was frankly an insult to their intelligence. Yet the question still remains as to why the police saw fit to continue with the charade themselves.

When he had dried himself and his clothes thoroughly, McGladdery was allowed to walk free again, with his RUC surveillance team picking him up as he left, of course.

The next day saw more and more police officers drafted in to search alongside the general public, who were volunteering in droves. By now the search area had been expanded to cover around four square miles, with every tree and bush, shed and outbuilding combed thoroughly. The Clanrye River was still an obvious focus for many of those in the police search team, though the painstaking dragging was proving to be a slow process. But it was still seen as the most likely place for the killer to have disposed of evidence, particularly the murder weapon.

The police were now appealing to anyone living in the greater Newry area to assist them by searching their own properties, lands and holdings, and many detected a sense of desperation in the request. Hundreds of people battled bitter winds and dropping temperatures during the daylight hours to poke and prod rabbit holes and crevices in tree trunks, committed to lending a hand in a search which as time passed looked ever more likely to prove fruitless.

The 31st of January was probably the most difficult day for the Gamble family and their close friends, as it was the day of Pearl's funeral. This solemn event would, however, both unite the town in grief and give much-needed momentum to the police campaign for assistance.

As heavy white clouds gathered in the sky, snow began to fall around the cortege as it made its way from Pearl's home at Upper Damolly to the church at Old Meeting House Green in Newry town. Hundreds of people lined the route, many of Pearl's friends and work colleagues among them, crying and hugging one another. The floral tributes were too many to count, and an open, crepe-draped lorry followed behind the funeral car laden with as many as it could carry.

Of the many black days Newry had seen and would go on to witness, this was surely among the worst: the funeral of a young woman, little more than a girl really, her family, grief-stricken and numb, following behind her modest coffin, desperately trying to make sense of what was happening to them.

Reverend Nathaniel Small, of Downshire Road Presbyterian Church, which the Gamble family attended, presided over the funeral service. Memories of Pearl as a young girl at school and later as a diligent employee were relayed to the many who graced the pews, and could be heard by those who stood outside the church, unable to get a space inside.

It would not take long for the minister to catalogue Pearl's years upon this earth, as her life seemed to have ended almost before it had really begun. Nevertheless, the tears shed by her friends and family were testament to the mark she had left upon them all. Reverend Small's every word echoed the thoughts of almost every person living in the town, when he vented his incredulity at what had befallen Pearl: 'It is hard to believe that there is a person of such wickedness in our community. It is hard to believe that anyone could do such a wicked, cruel and dastardly thing. We trust that the perpetrator of this awful crime will be quickly brought to justice.'

There was a challenge in his statement, a challenge to the police to hurry matters along and to bring it all to a speedy conclusion.

A few days later, having witnessed the hardship that the Gamble family were experiencing after losing Pearl, Reverend Small decided to introduce an appeal for funds to help them through what would prove difficult times. In those days often the children in a family who had managed to obtain work would be relied upon to make a financial contribution to the weekly household budget. In many cases theirs was the only income, since both parents were considered unemployable either by reason of their age or because they lacked the necessary skills. It is not clear just how much the Gambles had relied on

Pearl's income, but their plight was obvious enough to their minister at least.

The effects of Pearl's murder spread like ripples across a pond. Each day brought forth another appeal for assistance, but there was still no success in the hunt for missing evidence and people were becoming less and less comfortable in their home town. At night the streets were almost deserted and what few people there were moved about in the security of small groups. There was a killer about, after all, and until the police could come forward and tell them categorically that they had their man, few people, particularly young women, felt safe enough to walk around at night.

Day or night, the only real activity about the town was that of the numerous police personnel moving from one area to another, or going to or returning from the search of the fields. The logistics of transporting, feeding and providing sleeping quarters for large numbers of men and women were becoming a huge headache, and success was only achieved through the willing commitment and professionalism of the RUC rank and file.

Everyone was keen to move things along as quickly as possible, but because no stone could be left unturned, the pace of the search was torturously slow. Senior police officers pored over local Ordnance Survey maps, estimating the likely parameters of the appropriate search area. They knew roughly the time of death from witness statements and from the first examination of the body when it was found, and it was fairly safe to assume that the killer would still have been on foot after the attack. From those details they could work out the rough distance he could have covered in the time immediately after the attack up until daylight and the time the incident was reported, and this would give them a radius within which to concentrate. It was by no means an exact science, but it was a good starting point, and a structured search was always more beneficial than a hell-for-leather rummage. Of course there was the odd variable in such an area, and the one which caused them particular concern was the current of the Clanrye River.

On 1 February there was great anticipation when the police were contacted by a young textile worker named Noel O'Hare, who had been cycling home from work when he saw what he thought to be a bag containing a man's clothing floating in the river, close to the gas works in Newry. Marked and unmarked police cars rushed to the area and numerous officers scoured the foaming waters from both banks of the river as it meandered through the town. If the bag was there, and there was no reason to believe otherwise, they had to recover it before it reached the mouth of the lough, or it could be lost for ever. Eventually it was spotted within reach of the bank and retrieved for inspection. But what had seemed like a major breakthrough proved to be a false alarm and a disheartening distraction.

The number of constables now involved in the physical search had risen to around one hundred, some having been drafted in from as far as Larne, in County Antrim, on the east coast. All around the country resources were stretched, with the investigation into the murder of Police Constable Anderson at Rosslea still in its early stages and another hunt for a missing Portadown woman still demanding attention. Still, the fact that the press were relentless in giving column inches to the more negative aspects of the search for Pearl's killer spurred the police to achieve the quickest possible resolution. Manpower was what was required, and that was what was being provided in abundance.

But while a great deal of manpower was being directed towards the search, there were other enquiries to be carried out, and several detectives were busy doing just that. This was also the day that Detective Head Constable George Farrelly had accompanied Detective Sergeant Knox and Detective Constable McCullen on a visit to McGladdery's home in order to carry out a further search, and on speaking with Farrelly about his route home on the evening of the dance, the suspect had agreed to physically retrace his steps with him.

There is very little I can say about whether or not it was advisable to let McGladdery walk the route alongside a senior investigating officer at such a sensitive time for everyone involved. Naturally this took place in broad daylight, in full view of members of the general public going about their business as usual. It would be natural for them to put two and two together as to why McGladdery was being chaperoned so closely by a plain-clothed detective, and I can see how the public perception might have been that this would taint any trial. But what it did do for Farrelly and the case was provide more opportunities with which to trip up McGladdery once the trial eventually began.

Nevertheless, what I do believe was a serious flaw in Farrelly's decision-making that day was to allow the person whom the police regarded as their prime suspect to confront and question John Albert Wilson, the caretaker of the Orange Hall, about matters that had taken place at the dance on 27 January.

We know that at this point McGladdery had not been arrested for the murder, and as far as all were concerned he was helping the police with their enquiries, but the reality was somewhat different and Farrelly was well aware of that. Yet, despite this, he was willing to let McGladdery make a direct approach to a material witness. When Farrelly agreed that he could speak to the caretaker, and then took him up to the Wilsons' living quarters, where the couple were at the time, I believe he was playing a very dangerous game. Two innocent parties were about to be confronted by a man whom many in the town now considered to be a crazed killer, wholly unstable and extremely volatile.

There was the possibility that Wilson would find McGladdery so intimidating that he would agree with virtually anything he was asked, lending some credence to the suspect's story about when he had left the hall to make his way home. On a more sinister note, though, it also had to be considered that should he provide the answers which McGladdery did not want to hear, both he and his wife might be placed in danger.

Such a scenario would definitely not take place in modern policing. When a witness comes forward to provide information to the police during any investigation, particularly one involving a murder, that person's vulnerability is one of the first things to be considered. First and foremost the police have a duty of care to all members of the public and would never consider sacrificing anyone's safety just to bring about a successful prosecution.

Nowadays it would be unthinkable for the police to agree to any confrontation between a prime suspect and any witness, regardless of how important their evidence was in the greater scheme of the investigation. Even when a suspect has been brought before the court and has been lucky enough to be granted bail pending trial, there are usually stringent bail conditions attached to their release. Among other things, those conditions forbid the person awaiting trial from contacting or interfering with any witnesses directly involved in the case. Without such assurances in place, it is unlikely that any witnesses would ever come forward to assist in any police inquiry, and without the public belief in the protection of the law and its guardians, the criminal justice system would struggle to bring offenders before the courts, never mind have them convicted.

McGladdery asked Wilson if he remembered him being at the dance that night and then went on to pose other questions, but always using an open question to invite a spontaneous answer. 'What way was I dressed?', 'Was I drunk?' and so on. But when it came to the issue of the time at which he had said he left the hall to make his way home, he asked a closed question: 'Didn't I go out of the dance at ten to two?' More of a statement than a question, this was intended to suggest to Wilson the answer that McGladdery wanted but, unfortunately for him, the caretaker was adamant and steadfast when he replied, 'Well, earlier, twenty to two or about that.' It was just what McGladdery did not want to hear. Head Constable Farrelly was happy to make notes about the question-and-answer session at the hall, as he had seen fit to caution McGladdery earlier in the afternoon, and he would include all the details in his deposition.

After McGladdery had taken Farrelly on the journey

that he professed to have been his route home after the dance, they eventually returned to his house at 4 Damolly Terrace. It was mid-afternoon and Detective Sergeant Samuel Jeffrey, along with Detective Sergeant Knox and another colleague, Detective Sergeant McCullen, were still carrying out door-to-door enquiries. As the officers entered his house, McGladdery turned to Jeffrey and said, 'Sergeant, this is a terrible fix. It looks bad for me.' Realising that McGladdery was yet again in a talkative mood, Jeffrey cautioned him so that anything he did say could be used against him. But again McGladdery was looking for someone to sound off to and asked Jeffrey if he could call off the 'tail', saying that if he did so he would produce the clothing. So the charade continued, the same game being played again and again by a desperate man who was backing further and further into a corner. It was surely monotonous for Jeffrey and his colleagues, but this time, when the detective played his expected part and asked why McGladdery did not want to give up the clothes, McGladdery turned to him and replied, 'Right, I'll ring up Mr Curran, my lawyer, and if he tells me to do it, I'll take you to where they are hidden. Would you go as far as Belfast?'

For a moment or two Jeffrey was lost for words. But he recovered quickly and said that he would be willing to go anywhere to get the clothes. At this McGladdery took off across the street to McGuigan's shop, which was one of the few places to have a public telephone. A few moments afterwards he returned and said that the number was engaged but he would try it again later. Twenty agonising minutes later McGladdery went back across to the shop and rang the number again.

As they waited for his return, Jeffrey, Farrelly, Knox and McCullen must have thought that at last they could be getting somewhere, but at the same time a shadow of doubt about their prime suspect may have entered their heads. It was to be short-lived, however, for McGladdery returned after four or five minutes and said, 'My lawyer says I'm to say nothing and to tell you nothing.'

It had all been yet another waste of time and effort, and the four policemen left McGladdery's house deflated and angry. They could not be sure if he had even made a call to Luke Curran, and even if he had, the content of that call would have been subject to legal privilege even if referred to in court in any subsequent trial. All they could hope for was that the clothes would turn up in the ongoing search without McGladdery's help, and that his ridiculous antics would end there.

CHAPTER SIX
FIGHT OR FLIGHT

As the inquiry reached its seventh day without any sign of the suspect's missing clothing or the murder weapon, County Inspectors Ferris and Walker must have been considering their options should the items in question, which essentially could form the strongest part of their case, never be found. Along with all the personnel they could muster, more and more volunteers would appear every day to lend a hand, but still they were drawing a blank. The local firemen came out in force, as did many senior members of the 1st Newry Scout Group, a complete cross-section of the community united by a single goal.

Newry Police Station's telephone number, 2222, was posted throughout the streets and on walls and telegraph poles in outlying rural areas in anticipation of that one call which could provide them with the lead they so badly needed, but there was no new information of any great significance.

For those who could not get out and about but still wanted to keep abreast of any developments, the local newspaper, the *Newry Reporter*, provided a daily update. For the rest of the community, particularly those who either worked or shopped in or around the town centre, McGladdery and his posse of detectives were supplying countless hours of amusement. Wherever he went they followed, and should he stop to speak to someone they made sure that they spoke with them after he had gone. Some of the public began to believe that the police were now clutching at straws by continually following this man a full week after the murder. The inquiry team were single-minded, though, still clinging to the idea that anything McGladdery did or said could well be of significance.

Unfortunately this meant that he had to be watched constantly, and even more so when, on 3 February, the *Belfast Telegraph* reported that a court had sentenced Omagh man Patrick Gallagher to death for the murder of his wife at Mullaghmena the previous year. It was one of two high-profile murder cases, both of a domestic nature, to be documented in the newspapers at the time, and it must have been obvious to all, but particularly to Robert McGladdery, that the circumstances of Pearl's murder would almost certainly result in the passing of the death sentence for the person convicted of her killing.

As it was, Gallagher escaped the hangman's noose, which had been scheduled for 22 February 1961, after a successful appeal, but the trial of Samuel McLaughlin, which began on 6 February, did result in his receiving the death penalty later that year.

The prime suspect was now, more than ever, considered to be a serious flight risk. Just one slip-up by the surveillance team could result in his making a dash for the border, and there was a good chance that, should he decide to do so, he could make it before the police would even have had time to mobilise roadblocks at all the major border crossings, let alone the secondary routes. But even if they did, he could still so easily slip into Ireland over the many fields or ditches that crisscrossed the beautiful but rugged South Armagh landscape: routes proven successful in the past by smugglers and terrorists alike. There were no physical fences anywhere along the border, other than the odd rolling roadblock on the main vehicular routes, and no real markers distinguishing Northern Ireland from the Republic. Even during the turbulent times of the Troubles in the Seventies and Eighties the road signs or the colour of the telephone boxes were often the only clear indicators that you had crossed over from one country to the other.

It was likely to be a desperate cat-and-mouse game, but one which Ferris and Walker were determined to win. Surveillance was to be tightened up and McGladdery given less of a free rein.

On the Wednesday of that week, 8 February, McGladdery made his way down into the town to sign on as unemployed. Afterwards, around 2.10pm, he breezed into the Lido cafe in Hill Street, otherwise known as Fallone's, a popular meeting place at the time. Sitting beside the jukebox just inside the front door were a group of four men, all biding their time before they too had to sign on to qualify for their state benefits. Two brothers, Pat and John McGill, along with Billy Smith and Peter Larkin, sat talking over their table, until all heads turned to see the figure of the now infamous Robert McGladdery framed by the doorway. They all knew McGladdery in one way or another, and exchanged a nod or two with him, probably then wishing they hadn't when he offered to buy them coffee or tea and join their company. He was a hard man to refuse, and after a few minutes, laden with five cups of tea, he sat down at their table.

Both William 'Billy' Smith and Peter Larkin would later provide detailed statements to the police about the meeting in Fallone's, and the interesting part of both statements is just how comfortable McGladdery is when talking to the men about the ongoing murder investigation of which he is the prime suspect. He does not avoid the subject at all, but instead seeks to draw them into the conversation and attempts to spin the same excuse for not handing in the clothes that he has already told to the police. It is apparent that McGladdery wanted to shape public opinion as much as possible, even to the extent of courting the local press in the form of the *Newsletter* and nationally the *Daily Mail*. His arrogance knew no boundaries and he seemed to bask in his local 'celebrity'. As he invited questions from the press he was still very willing to admit involvement in a degree of criminal activity, while in each interview distancing himself from Pearl's murder.

I am not sure his solicitor, Luke Curran, would have approved of his giving any statements to journalists, but then again I believe that Mr Curran may have had little if any control over his client at the time. When the *Belfast Telegraph* spoke with McGladdery on 9 February he made the following statement: 'I have been asked to produce the clothing I was wearing on that night. If given 24 hours freedom from police interference, I will turn up the clothes worn by me on that night, otherwise they will not be turned up. These clothes will prove me innocent of the crime.'

Some would say that the papers were naive in

granting McGladdery any space at all, thus affording him some sort of credibility. But the fact is that whichever way the story would end for McGladdery, they would have got exactly what they wanted – either an interview with an innocent man harassed by the police, or an interview with a crazed killer. Either way, it was good for sales.

When McGladdery had finished spinning his yarn about the clothes to Larkin and the rest, he asked them if they could organise a taxi to meet him in Mill Street beside Boyle's fruit shop. He told them he needed it so that he could go and fetch the clothes from where he had hidden them, explaining that if he got them he could clear the whole thing up by that coming Saturday. He also said that if Mr Fallone would let him leave by the back door he would give him a pound.

It was all a bit desperate, and not one of the four were taken in by the story in any way, and certainly not enough to go out and order the taxi for him. Realising that they had no intention of helping him out, McGladdery turned his attention instead to two young women seated elsewhere in the cafe.

When the police caught up with the four men and were given an account of the conversation the quartet had just had with their prime suspect, they could sense that he was becoming more desperate – he was going to make a run for it.

There were a few developments over the period of 7–9 February which seemed to require most of the witnesses who had already been spoken to being revisited by detectives. The papers reported on 7 February that the police were following a 'new' line of enquiry, the nature of which was not made clear. All they were able to say was that the clothes had still not been located. It had to be considered that the police were now beginning to play McGladdery at his own game, trying to force his hand by suggesting they were making some progress: they had a lead maybe, or a witness who could steer them towards the clothes. There was nothing to lose by doing so. Up until then McGladdery had seemed too cocky and hadn't shown any signs of breaking under the pressure of constant surveillance. The question was whether he would now take the bait and go back to where he had hidden the clothes, or would he run?

On the evening of 9 February at around 8.45 Constable Donald Keown was standing in Hill Street. Stamping his feet to ward off the cold and blowing into his gloved hands, he watched as Robert McGladdery exited Fallone's cafe with a few other men and walked up to the Savoy cinema in Monaghan Street. He could tell it was going to be a long night, settling into a position from which he could watch the front door of the cinema, confident that the rear exit was being covered by a colleague.

When the feature film had ended, McGladdery and his cronies came out and walked back along Hill Street to Fallone's. They stayed there until just before midnight, when McGladdery left the cafe with one other man and they began walking through the town towards the Belfast Road. The two stopped at Trevor Hill, where they talked for around five minutes before parting at 12.05.

Until then Constable Keown had not been at all concerned about McGladdery's behaviour, but as the two men went their opposite ways McGladdery broke into a run, speeding up further as he passed the courthouse. Keown tried in vain to keep up with his charge, but McGladdery was just too fast and he lost sight of him near the Scriptural Hall in Downshire Road at 12.10.

It was the worst possible scenario, letting the suspect give him the slip in the middle of the night. Keown's first instinct was to continue up the Belfast Road to Damolly Lane, which eventually would lead to McGladdery's house, and confirm that he had not made it that far. He did so, but not before relaying a message back to the station. On his way out to Damolly Lane, Keown saw no one. Panic must have been setting in, and the young constable must have been wondering exactly how he was going to tell his superiors that he was responsible for letting Robert McGladdery escape.

Just as soon as news that McGladdery had taken to his heels reached Newry Police Station, Constable Thom was dispatched in his own car to drive along the Belfast Road and assist Keown. It would have been 12.25 by the time Thom was briefed about what had happened, and he didn't lose a moment in making his way out in the direction of Damolly. Fortunately he spotted McGladdery walking along the footpath on the left-hand side of the Belfast Road, a good distance ahead of Constable Keown, and only some 375 yards from the entrance into the village on the Newry side. He passed the walking figure and drove on, before turning his vehicle around at the entrance to Damolly Lane and coming back on the route he had just driven. This time, however, he did not see McGladdery on the footpath or in the road. Where had he gone?

Again Thom turned around and went back in the direction of the village, and even as far as McGladdery's house, but there was still no sign of him.

Both policemen must have breathed a sigh of relief, however, when at 12.45am, Keown spotted McGladdery coming along Damolly Lane to his house. The burning question now was, where exactly had the suspect gone in the time between 12.25, the last occasion he was spotted by Thom, and 12.45, when Keown saw him walking down the lane towards the row of terraced houses?

There had to be some reason why McGladdery had taken off as he had, and there was always the possibility that he had risen to the bait and had gone to make sure that what he had hidden had not been disturbed. The police couldn't afford not to search the area, even though they knew their man had played such games before and may have been trying to steer them away from the focus of the main search. The next day DS Jeffrey and a few others were sent to scout out the area close to where Thom had last seen McGladdery before he disappeared the previous night. At around 11am Jeffrey entered a field behind five houses fronting the Newry Road and running alongside Damolly Lane. As he walked slowly through the field, close to a ditch at the edge furthermost from the Damolly Lane side, he came across a large concrete slab on the ground, which on closer inspection he found to be a septic tank. There were two openings, one at each end, and both were covered by concrete blocks. The slab itself was over 16 feet long by 7? feet wide, and the blocks were 31 inches square. It took some effort, but Jeffrey moved the block covering the opening closest to the ditch, and with the aid of a stick from the hedge began the dirty job of poking around in the liquid in the tank. It wasn't long before he felt something bulky yet 'soft' in the bottom corner, and with the assistance of other police officers and a grappling hook he was able to remove the item after only a few failed attempts.

Police work can be a less than glamorous job, especially when you end up rooting through other people's rubbish, or worse still human waste, during a search. But if the end result is as good as it was for Jeffrey that morning, it is a task that no police officer would mind doing every day of his career. Out of the depths of the septic tank came a bag, the neck of which was tightly knotted. It was tied so tightly that Jeffrey decided to clear a patch on the concrete slab and cut it open with his penknife. Later examinations of the 'bag' by a forensic scientist suggest that, although extremely heavily soiled, it may in fact have been a pillowcase. Whatever it was, what came out of it first was a tightly rolled-up overcoat, fawn-coloured and in the 'shortie' style, with leather buttons and epaulettes on the shoulders and a tab on the inside saying 'All Wool Showerproof'. When he opened out the overcoat further and examined it, Jeffrey found large patches of reddish-brown staining on the left and right shoulders and around the collar. It had to be McGladdery's coat. Along with the shortie coat in the bag were other items, all of which bore what appeared to be blood staining. These items included a blue undervest, a white handkerchief, a red-and-black striped tie in two halves and a pair of black leather shoes with rubber soles. Although clearly excited by the find, Jeffrey was concerned that there was no sign of the light-blue suit amongst the bag's contents.

At the bottom of what later appeared to be a pillowcase there was a large stone which had been used to weigh it down and which seemed to have come from a wall beside the tank.

When he had finished laying out all the items and labelling them with their sequential exhibit marks, Jeffrey set about pacing out the distance from the tank to Damolly Lane and then from the tank to the houses lying on the Newry Road. When he paced out a route which would lead him to Damolly Lane and then on to McGladdery's house, it proved to be 376 paces.

McGladdery had hidden the clothes almost within sight of his own front door, in a place he knew well enough to have remembered there was a septic tank.

The whole team of detectives were elated when news of Jeffrey's find made its way back to the station. This was just the break they were looking for, and after all the criticism they had received and the many hours of exhaustive surveillance and searching, they decided not to waste any more time with McGladdery. As far as they were concerned, they now had enough evidence to pick him up and hold him for further questioning, and put an end to his game.

While the station was the scene of congratulatory handshakes and back-slapping, some officers were still carrying out their enquiries, oblivious to the latest developments. Detective Sergeant Charles Hunter was standing in Damolly at midday talking with William McGuigan, the owner of the local shop across the way from McGladdery's house, when he saw the suspect come to the front door and beckon him over. McGladdery then said something to Hunter along the lines of, 'Sergeant, you didn't get those clothes yet?' Hunter replied that he did not know, and before continuing on cautioned McGladdery, reminding him that he would be writing down the contents of their conversation.

Unconcerned about this, McGladdery replied, 'I know that, but I want to tell you now. You'll not get the clothes in the North of Ireland. They're in the State,' – the Republic of Ireland was, and often still is, referred to as the 'Free State' by some – 'and what's more, starting from tonight, if I don't get 24 hours' freedom from police escort, I'll give an order, in fact I have given an order, for the clothes to be destroyed. I'll assume they are not got yet, if you have got them it must have been since last night, any time after midnight, that's all I want to say.'

There was something odd about this rant of McGladdery's. I think he knew that the police had been close behind him the previous night, and possibly believed that he may have even compromised his hiding place. Had he been just sitting at home expecting a knock on the door at any time, and when it hadn't come had he grown more and more agitated and confused? Whatever the truth, there is a sense of desperation in what he said, and a feeling that he knew he was almost at the end of the road, and that he may even have been relieved if that were the case.

He didn't have to wait too long, though, for at 1.10pm on 10 February 1961 Detective Sergeants Jeffrey and Gibson knocked on the door of 4 Damolly Terrace and took Robert Andrew McGladdery into custody to answer further questions.

For any investigator, just knowing that you are about to confront your suspect with evidence which is undeniably damning can be the most satisfying feeling. Every 'copper' likes to have the upper hand, an ace in the deck, even if it is just a single piece of evidence which the suspect will not be able to explain away.

No solicitor is recorded as being present with McGladdery that afternoon when at 2.45 District Inspector Bradley walked into the interview room at Newry Police Station and introduced himself to the lean young man seated nervously behind the little table. Nor was the interview tape-recorded, for these were the days when every record of conversations between interrogator and suspect was handwritten. Even without a tape to set the scene, one can easily imagine the tension in the room. Along with him, DI Bradley had brought four exhibits marked 'B.M.', 'B.N.', 'B.P.' and 'B.S.', the items which had been removed from the septic tank. The suspect was then cautioned and the items were shown to him. As they were placed in front of him on the table, Bradley remembered, McGladdery glanced at the clothes, then drew back his head and gasped. According to Bradley, the suspect turned 'rather pale'. The game was well and truly over.

At 4.10pm that same day, a full two weeks after Pearl Gamble's murder, McGladdery was read the charge: 'You, Robert Andrew McGladdery, on 28 January 1961, at Damolly, Newry, in the County of Down, did murder Pearl Gamble.' The caution he then received afforded him a chance to reply, but all he could muster was, 'Nothing to say,' a sharp contrast from someone who had been so vocal before.

The moment of charge was, I am sure, a relief for all involved in the investigation: detectives, constables and searchers alike. But, more importantly, it must have been even more of a relief for Pearl's family, who during those two weeks after her murder had had to come to terms in some way with the fact that the prime suspect was parading throughout the very town they lived in, flaunting himself at every occasion. It must have been heartbreaking for them to read the stories in the paper, to see just how slowly the investigation was moving and to face the possibility that the vital pieces of evidence which were being sought may never surface. I do not believe that there were any triumphant celebrations in their household when the police called to inform them that they had charged McGladdery with Pearl's murder. More likely, a few tears were shed as at last they were able to set aside uncertainty and bitterness and begin grieving as a family.

For the police, the task now was to bring McGladdery before the first available court and have him remanded in custody so that all the evidence could be assessed and the case against him could be built step by step.

Compiling a case file for trial was something that was not going to be done in a few days. To date over 50 witnesses had been involved in the case, and every one of their statements had to be sorted through, amendments made and agreed, and their personal details recorded. Not only that, but an extensive list of exhibits had been collected during each part of the investigation, all of which had been given an identifiable mark, and these had then to be presented in such a way that it would be easy to read where and when they were found and seized, and by whom.

From the very first item recovered by the police during the investigation, a pair of ladies' stiletto-heeled shoes which had been given the police mark 'A', right through to the sheet from McGladdery's bed, marked 'CD', 69 items in all had to be carefully examined by a forensic scientist, who would then be asked to present his or her findings during the forthcoming court case. It would be a painstaking process, but a very necessary one in terms of linking the available physical evidence to the involvement of the suspect.

The responsibility for this task fell to Derek McVitty BSc of the forensic science laboratory at Belfast's Verner Street, and it would be several weeks before he would be in a position to present his findings.

There are stark contrasts between the capabilities of forensic science of the early Sixties and those we recognise today, and these are very apparent when one reads the findings in McVitty's report concerning the exhibits in this case. There is no suggestion that he was anything but thorough, for I believe that he subjected every single exhibit he was passed to the most rigorous of tests, but rather that the technology available at that time for determining close similarities between samples such as hair and blood was vague in its results compared with those possible today.

During his examination of Pearl's clothing and personal effects, along with other items found at the scene, McVitty makes reference to numerous stains of type 'O' blood, which, when compared with a sample of Pearl's own blood, also confirmed as type 'O', was assumed to have originated from her. The only other important blood sample is the one taken later from McGladdery himself, which turns out to be of type 'A'.

One would have thought that it would have been fairly straightforward to first examine the clothing recovered from the septic tank, and after proving beyond a doubt that these items did in fact belong to Robert McGladdery, match the blood which had thoroughly stained the garments with Pearl's blood. In this way the connection between killer and victim would have been made.

Today that would almost certainly be the procedure, but back then McVitty was hampered by the simple fact that DNA comparison was a thing of the distant future, and at that time all he could realistically be sure of was the group to which the blood belonged – type 'O', type 'A' and so on – but not whose blood it actually was.

In fact it would be a full quarter of a century, 1986 to be precise, when DNA profiling as we know it would first be used in a criminal case. After ground-breaking work at the University of Leicester during the Seventies the process of identifying individuals through their DNA was finely tuned and adapted to enable law-enforcement agencies around the world to quickly link a potential suspect with a particular crime. As technology rapidly advances, the time it takes to process DNA samples is being reduced considerably, with researchers at the University of Hull even closer to producing a portable profiling device, which might mean an analysis could be produced in just an hour, as opposed to between one and two days.

For McVitty and his colleagues working in forensic science laboratories across the world in the Sixties, like-for-like comparisons were as good as it got. Blood, hair, saliva and sperm samples collected at a crime scene and compared had to be described in their reports in terms of 'similarity', which in the justice system of the time was acceptable evidence. It would be the prosecution's job to present that evidence to the jury, along with the origins of those samples, and let them draw their own conclusions.

On the day of his arrest and charge McGladdery was brought before the Crown Court in Newry by DI Bradley and remanded in custody until 22 February to allow the police time to present their case. Effectively this appearance was to determine if the police considered they had enough evidence to be able to connect the defendant to the charge, and Bradley was confident that they had.

It is not uncommon for a person accused, whether in custody or not, to wait a considerable time to have their day in court in the form of a trial. In the meantime, though, they may have to appear before a lesser court on several occasions before that trial commences. The reason is simply that this allows everyone, prosecution and defence alike, time to prepare their case and to make final enquiries.

On each occasion at which McGladdery appeared in court, DI Bradley would insist on the suspect being further remanded in custody until the next proposed court date, bearing in mind the nature of the crime and the associated risks of the accused taking flight from the jurisdiction, among other things.

There was never any real possibility of McGladdery being released at this stage, but under the rule of law he was entitled to protest, through his legal representative, at being held in custody at each and every appearance he made.

On 22 February McGladdery was taken in a grey prison van from Belfast to Newry to appear before the Crown Court. Almost all traffic in Trevor Hill came to a standstill as a crowd of six or seven hundred people gathered at 10am in anticipation of his arrival. There was a half-hearted cheer when the van arrived, swung around in the forecourt and backed up to the steps of the courthouse. A police cordon had been organised to keep the crowd back from the building, and earlier had restricted entry to the court to those on official business. Nevertheless, 11 women and 17 men had managed to secure their place in the body of the court, intent on observing proceedings.

As McGladdery and his escort stepped swiftly from the back of the van and up the main steps, the crowd surged forward, eager to get a look at the killer and voice their disgust. Never one to disappoint an audience, McGladdery had insisted on wearing a black suit and cerise shirt, topped off with a grey pork-pie hat, and while in the dock chatted freely with the guard he had been handcuffed to.

It was obvious to all that during McGladdery's appearance, and just two weeks after his arrest, his solicitor, Luke Curran, was intent on setting out his stall. When Bradley asked for a further 14 days' remand, Curran questioned his legal authority, and was told it was being made under the provisions of the Petty Sessions and Summary Jurisdiction Act. Bradley was pressed further by the solicitor as to the precise section, leaving Mr Moore of the Crown Prosecution Service no option but to hurry to his office to retrieve the relevant copy of the Act.

Not content to stop there, Curran probed Bradley on the availability of his witnesses, and was told that none but himself was present in court. For some reason he kept asking Bradley if there were any witnesses not available because they were out of the jurisdiction, by which he probably meant Northern Ireland as a whole, and said that if this was so he could not proceed with the case. Of course, the reality was that two weeks was nowhere near enough time for the prosecution to have fully investigated the case, and Bradley had seen no reason why he should have asked any of the witnesses to attend as he did not intend to proceed on that day.

It was clear that Curran was going to play hardball

with the prosecution, giving them notice that their case would have to be solid and absolutely watertight. The rules of engagement were being drawn up.

After his cross-examination of Bradley, Curran turned to the Magistrate to remonstrate, saying, 'An offence was committed approximately a month ago and McGladdery has been in custody for almost two weeks. During that time enquiries have been made and I submit it is the duty of the prosecution to proceed with their case against him as soon as is possible. A man has been deprived of his liberty and put on the peril of his life and all we hear is that at some unspecified date the Crown will be prepared to proceed. I submit that either the prosecution should give an undertaking to proceed at an early stage or else the accused should be entitled to his liberty. I oppose on his behalf and instruct him to object to any prolonged adjournments. It is his right to do so, and I feel the court will protect the liberty of the subject and see that he is put forward for trial, or cleared and let go free at the earliest.'

It was a theatrical performance, and one which was rounded off by his client's robust reply of 'No! No, Your Worship' when asked if he consented to a remand until 7 March. The outcome was a further remand until 1 March: less than had been requested but a minor victory for Curran nonetheless.

As the hearing came to a conclusion almost 30 minutes later, the crowd outside, which had swollen to around a thousand, waited impatiently for a glimpse of McGladdery. When he finally appeared, now wearing his pork-pie hat, a large jeer went up and there were many angry shouts and pointed fingers. McGladdery just laughed and gave the 'thumbs up' sign, stirring the crowd into a frenzy of abuse, with women spitting venomously at the van as it slowly moved out into the traffic, heading back in the direction of the Crumlin Road Prison in north Belfast.

It would be 19 April before all the depositions would be completed at a special court in Newry, and on that appearance McGladdery was returned for trial to Down Spring Assizes on 1 May.

This was to be the date for his preliminary examination, or P.E., at which a 'True Bill' was returned and an application was made by his own counsel for an adjournment to the Autumn Assizes. The 'True Bill' was a formal way of declaring that the court believed that there was a case for the defendant to answer and a prosecution to be pursued.

From what I can determine, the stages of a Crown case today are very similar to those of the Sixties. First there is the initial appearance to answer the charge and for the investigating officer to connect the defendant to the charge. At the P.E. stage the investigating officer hands a primary disclosure pack to the defendant's solicitor, and later, on arraignment – that is, when the defendant is formally accused or indicted – a date for trial is agreed after availability of witnesses has been established.

It would be six months before McGladdery's trial date would arrive, a lengthy period for him to have to spend on remand, but realistically his own counsel would need all of that time if they were to prepare the defence.

We know that McGladdery had actively courted the press all the while he was the prime suspect in the case, and at every opportunity had expressed his innocence and his desire to be given the freedom to recover the clothes he had worn without the presence of a police surveillance team. But it wasn't only the local papers that had shown an interest: the story was much bigger and had captured the imagination of the dailies on the mainland. On 9 February, just a day before the clothes were discovered by the police, and right in the middle of the investigation, the *Daily Mail* and the *Daily Express* each ran a story about McGladdery and the bizarre murder hunt surrounding him. At its best this was sensationalism in what must have been a slow week for news, but the stories were to have far-reaching implications.

Not only were large photographs of the man of the moment printed prominently, but he was also described by the *Daily Mail* as a 'self confessed gunman, safe cracker, thief and general desperado'. The same paper printed snippets of an interview with McGladdery, along with descriptions of how large crowds appeared to follow his every movement about the town, along with his ever-present police chaperone. All very entertaining for the reader, but potentially damning in terms of tainting public opinion.

There was no doubt that the details published could be damaging to any potential court case, and as expected, both publications were immediately challenged by the Divisional Court in Belfast. After deliberation, fines in excess of £7,000, a huge sum of money back in 1961, were imposed upon the *Express* and the *Mail*, with the ruling describing their reports as 'calculated to prejudice his [McGladdery's] trial'.

Lingering in the air was the suggestion that McGladdery had been paid for his efforts, but they were never confirmed, regardless of his bragging to several people about having secured payment for his story.

The newspapers' stories certainly proved expensive for the publishers, but they also unwittingly provided some purchase for McGladdery as he languished in Crumlin Road awaiting trial. Never one to miss out on an opportunity, he penned a letter to the Central Criminal Court in London: a confusing rant about just how much he believed the stories had undermined any opportunity he may have had of receiving a fair and unbiased trial at the hands of a jury from Northern Ireland. His demands were far from clear, not only because he was addressing his complaints to another jurisdiction entirely, but because he worded his objections in a manner which would have been difficult for anyone other than himself to decipher. What was blatantly explicit, though, was his 'demand' at the end of the letter to be exonerated of the murder charge because of the newspapers' impropriety. He was either extremely naive or badly informed, but the newspaper articles, although damaging, would by no means have any great sway in securing his release. Even when he quoted the then Attorney General, Sir William Brian Maginess, who had always expressed concern about any media attention during murder investigations, his words fell on deaf ears.

Now confined to prison awaiting his trial, McGladdery quickly realised that he was powerless to assert any influence over matters happening outside. He was in regular contact with his solicitor, Luke Curran, and his barrister, James Brown QC, but he was becoming more and more impatient and disgruntled. In a letter dated 7 September of that year, addressed to the offices of Luke Curran, McGladdery appears ready to dismiss his legal team and conduct his own defence. For reasons known only to himself, McGladdery, being unhappy with his treatment in jail, holds his own counsel responsible for not addressing his position.

He actually names another inmate, L.V. Henderson, as the cause of his annoyance simply because he believes that Henderson was receiving preferential treatment from prison staff because he was said to be the nephew of the then Lord Mayor of Belfast. Being fairly well acquainted with prison rules, McGladdery believed that Henderson, who was in jail under 'preventative detention', was not entitled to a radio or other privileges he was enjoying. Whether there was any truth in the allegations was not made clear: only that Henderson was confined to the prison hospital at that time, and conditions there were said to have been less harsh than for the other inmates.

Whatever happened over the coming weeks in September, McGladdery was made to see sense and Curran and Brown continued to represent him in the lead-up to the trial. The feeling of losing control may have been what he feared most, that and the fact that the press had not so much as mentioned his name in the run-up to the trial, perhaps causing his irritation. In the events immediately following the murder and for many weeks after, McGladdery had almost been a household name, but now other, more important things were making the headlines and he would have to wait until October to grace the front pages again.

CHAPTER SEVEN

TRIAL AND APPEAL

Despite attempts by Luke Curran at the end of June to have the trial moved to Londonderry or Fermanagh, or for that matter anywhere other than County Down or County Armagh, the trial began without delay on 9 October. It was generally accepted that any case, not just McGladdery's, would have some risk of prejudice in respect of partisanship, but in his particular circumstances there was little evidence to support any great degree of such feeling. There was certainly ill will towards him, but between February and October people had been busy getting on with their own lives. It was only the resurrection of events by the press every now or then which revived such strong emotions in the community.

When 9 October eventually came around the Crown's

case against McGladdery was placed in the safe hands of the Right Honourable W.B. Maginess QC, ably assisted by Mr C. Nicholson QC, and Mr R. Babbington BL, under the instructions of the Crown's solicitor, Mr W.T.J. Bradley. It was an intimidating line-up, and the defence team, comprising Mr James Brown QC, alongside Mr Turlough O'Donnell BL, and instructed by Luke Curran, knew that their task was far from easy.

William Brian Maginess, usually known as Brian Maginess, had been a well-known figure in Northern Ireland for some years, and in 1961 held the position of Attorney General, a post he would fill until his appointment as a County Court judge in 1964. A graduate in law of Trinity College, Dublin, he was called to the bar in 1923, with the only major interruption in his career being the Second World War, when he served his country in the Royal Corps of Artillery.

Maginess's interest in local politics saw him fight and win the Lisburn seat of Iveagh in 1938, and after returning from action in 1945 he served as Minister of Labour, Minister of Home Affairs and Minister of Finance in the Northern Ireland Government of Sir Basil Brooke. Such was the esteem in which he was held that many tipped him to succeed Brooke as Prime Minister in the North.

Unfortunately, in the early Fifties Maginess alienated himself from the rank and file of the Orange Institution when he made a ruling banning particular Orange marches through Nationalist areas in County Down and County Londonderry. Bearing in mind the stranglehold the Orange tradition had over many of the political decisions made by the Northern Ireland Government at the time, Brooke had no choice but to appease them and remove Maginess from the cabinet, and he was then appointed to the Attorney General's post.

That wasn't Maginess's only brush with the Unionist community, though, as in 1959 he was lambasted by none other than Ian Paisley for his speech at an Ulster Young Unionist Council event where he openly supported Catholic membership of the Ulster Unionist Party. His dismissal was called for during an Ulster Protestant Action demonstration at Stormont Castle led by Paisley himself, but it would not be until 1964, more than two years after the McGladdery case, that he voluntarily resigned from Parliament.

Presiding over the trial would be Lord Justice Major Sir Lancelot Curran, himself a former Attorney General for Northern Ireland during the late Forties, and a Unionist party member and lifetime Orangeman. He was himself a controversial figure for more than one reason. It was rumoured that he had accrued large gambling debts at the Ulster Reform Club, a pastime frowned upon by many of his colleagues in the judiciary as it was thought it could compromise his position. But almost ten years before the McGladdery trial was to begin, Lord Justice Curran's family were suffering a tragedy of their own, and one which in some ways mirrored the murder of Pearl Gamble.

On 13 November 1952 Lord Justice Curran's daughter Patricia was discovered, by her 26-year-old brother Desmond, murdered in the grounds of their family home, The Glen, in the Belfast suburb of Whiteabbey. Like Pearl, she was only 19 and was a student at the city's Queen's University. The facts of the case were that Patricia was found at around 1.50am, and had been stabbed 37 times. She was last seen at around 5.20pm the previous day a short distance from her home after getting off a bus from Belfast, just five miles away.

When a policeman arrived at the scene some ten minutes later, he complied with Judge Curran's suggestion that the body be transported at once by car to a doctor's surgery, and he was assisted in this by the judge, his son Desmond and the family's solicitor. It was an unusual set of circumstances, and when the area where the body was found was finally searched for evidence it became apparent that, despite the number of wounds inflicted on Patricia, there was surprisingly little blood. It was clear to all that she had been murdered elsewhere and her body moved. This, along with the fact that the judge refused police entry to his house to search for over a week, made for an even more bizarre investigation.

Although it had been raining heavily that night, items of an 'evidential' nature, such as her books and a beret, were found about ten yards away from where her body had lain, but in contrast with Patricia and her clothing they were dry. The police launched an extensive investigation during which several thousand witness statements were recorded. But it would be a full two months before a 'prime suspect' was identified, in the form of a Scottish RAF man named Iain Hay Gordon.

This rather timid and 'odd' character had actually been an acquaintance of Desmond Curran, and when arrested in January 1953 he was grilled by senior investigating officers over three long days. The interrogation was carried out without the presence of Gordon's legal representative, and the means used during the marathon session were described as 'ruthless', unsurprisingly producing a confession from Gordon.

During the trial, on 2 March 1953, Lord Justice McDermott ruled the confession as admissible and, despite any forensic evidence, Gordon faced the hangman's noose. The defence team then introduced a plea of insanity and based the rest of the trial on evidencing Gordon's condition. A verdict of guilty by virtue of insanity was duly returned by the jury, and the convicted man was committed to a mental institution in

Antrim, where over the next seven years he never received any medication for his 'condition' and, on his release in 1960, was considered sane.

Some time later Desmond Curran, a trained barrister, converted to Catholicism, took Holy Orders to become a priest and secured a position with the missionaries in South Africa. Iain Hay Gordon went on to campaign every single day after his release to have his name cleared of the murder, and the Criminal Cases Review Commission succeeded in having the 'confession' thrown out as plausible admissible evidence by the Court of Appeal in July 2000.

Acting for McGladdery and instructed by his solicitor, Luke Curran, was James Brown QC. Curran's practice was situated in Newry town centre and it is likely, judging by McGladdery's offending history, that he had acted on his behalf on a number of occasions before. Brown may also have considered himself a 'local', as he had attended primary school at Mourne Grange in nearby Kilkeel. He broke away from those early roots by continuing his education at Campbell College in Belfast and then Oxford University, where he was an important figure in the Oxford Union. Those who knew him remembered him as a great orator, a large man with a commanding presence but a likeable disposition. During the Second World War he had seen active service, and had returned home nursing a wound which troubled him thereafter. His father was Thomas Watters Brown, Unionist MP for North Down in the Twenties, a High Court judge in later life and the last man to have held the post of Solicitor General for Ireland, until August 1921, when the position was scrapped with the coming inception of the Irish Free State in 1922. Long after the McGladdery case was over, James followed his father into the judiciary, first becoming a County Court judge in Down and then the Recorder in Belfast.

Because the trial was being held in Downpatrick, 25 miles from Newry, it was always going to be a logistical nightmare making sure that all 59 witnesses were at hand when required to give their evidence. A bus was laid on to convey them to the courthouse each day and return them to Newry afterwards. All eyes were on the accused as he arrived that first morning, 9 October 1961, from the Crumlin Road jail, dressed in a dark suit and handcuffed to both of his prison escorts.

The preliminaries of the trial began in earnest at noon, when the accused and both prosecution and defence counsels were present during the selection of the jury. It was no surprise to anyone that the jury would be made up of 12 males, considering the crime had been committed against a female, and just as soon as they had been chosen they were informed by Judge Curran that they were to be sequestered for the term of the trial. Hurried telephone calls were made to relatives, and police officers duly dispatched to the jurors' homes to collect clothes and toiletries to last them at least a week. It was unlikely that there were any concerns about jury tampering, but it was normal to protect jurors involved in a capital murder case where the outcome could mean the death penalty. For the duration of the trial all 12 men and their chaperones would stay overnight in the seaside town of Bangor, but for them it would be anything but a holiday.

Before the jury took their places in the court, Mr Brown first made a submission to the judge regarding eight particular photographs in the album supplied by the police. These eight photographs were of Pearl Gamble's deceased remains and were described by Brown as 'extremely distressing'. It was his opinion that they could be prejudicial to his client and therefore he wished that they be excluded from evidence. The photographs were considered important by the prosecution as they believed they could assist the jury in understanding certain aspects of the assault on the victim. There were no elements in the photographs relating to 'defensive wounds', and Judge Curran had to consider the need to include them at all. In the end he ruled that the photographs were not of evidential value to either the prosecution or the defence but may indeed prove prejudicial. They were to be excluded.

And so the prosecution, in the form of the Attorney

General William Maginess, began by outlining the case against the accused and stating how he intended to show beyond doubt that Robert McGladdery was responsible for the brutal murder of Pearl Gamble. The jury were first given the background of the dance on the evening of 27 January 1961, then the events as they had unfolded, with the accused stealing a bicycle from outside the Orange Hall and making his way to the Upper Damolly crossroads to lay in wait for his victim. The ferocious attack on Pearl was described in detail and then the jury were told of the efforts the accused had made to hide evidence and remove any traces of involvement from the crime. Maps of the crime scene in relation to Pearl's house, the Orange Hall, McGladdery's house and the septic tank were then distributed among the jurors. It was important for them to be able to see the geography of the area in the context of the events and to be able to gauge distances.

The Attorney General made no bones about the fact that the prosecution's case was mostly circumstantial, though, in his words, it was 'none the worse for it'. He intended to show the jury that there were no other explanations for McGladdery not being able to turn up the missing clothes other than he had not wanted to incriminate himself in the murder of Pearl Gamble.

The first witnesses to be called were Charles Ashe and Bob McCullough, who both painted a picture of the morning of 28 January, when they had come across the discarded and bloodstained clothing at the scene of the attack. As far as the defence was concerned there was little point in cross-examination as their evidence was plain and simple.

The opening day was very much less newsworthy than most would have imagined. Naturally the defence team had a strategy, but what exactly it was didn't surface until Day Two.

At the start of the second morning the prosecution made Judge Curran aware that one of their witnesses, Maud Wilson, the wife of the caretaker at the Orange Hall, would not be appearing as she was suffering from anxiety and depression. The Attorney General considered submitting an application to Judge Curran to have her testimony accepted in her absence, but abandoned the idea. She was not necessarily a 'key' witness, after all, and there were plenty of others there to cover the points he needed in terms of McGladdery's movements and mode of dress that evening.

On the morning of the 10th, Head Constable O'Hara took the witness box to face questions from both teams. The first exhibits he was asked to identify were those which he had seen on the morning of 28 January in the kitchen of Pearl's house, the two pairs of shoes and the various bits of clothing which her mother, Margaret Gamble, had collected up. The bicycle which had been recovered at the crossroads was wheeled into the court and other soiled pieces of Pearl's clothing laid out in front of O'Hara for consideration. The prosecution then referred to the cuts on McGladdery's face which O'Hara had mentioned in his statement, and their prominence on the evening of 28 January when he had spoken to McGladdery at the station at around 10pm. The explanation McGladdery had given him about the accident with the chest expanders was relayed by O'Hara, and the prosecution saw no reason to continue questions.

All that Brown could offer as a counter was to ask O'Hara, who was well aware of the police presence surrounding McGladdery during every part of the investigation, if he concurred that such a presence could be described as 'alarming and unnerving', as Brown so believed it to have been. O'Hara said that he did not concur.

The next witness in the box was Pearl's mother, who must have been thankful when Judge Curran decided to spare her the trauma of identifying the clothing exhibits, taking it for granted that the defence would have no objection.

As anyone who has ever given evidence in a court will know, it is a daunting experience, even for the more experienced police officer. Every question asked seems designed to catch you out and your every answer is dissected at length. The counsel's job is to chip away at the fabric of the testimony the witness has provided and undermine the reliability and credibility of that evidence. But, to Margaret Gamble's credit, she remained resolute and focused when she told the packed courtroom that she had known Robert McGladdery for quite some years, around the time his family had lived at Tinker Hill in fact. She was clear in her recollection that he had even been in her house some 12 years or so before.

It would have been a mistake for Brown or his team to consider an aggressive cross-examination of Mrs Gamble. Like it or not, they were going to have to accept that she had presented the jury with the first real contradiction of their client's story. McGladdery had always claimed that he had no idea where Pearl had lived: 'somewhere in the country' was about as close as he got. But there it was for all to hear: he had known all the time exactly where she lived.

As each independent witness was called, the question as to what the accused had been wearing at the dance was the one which the prosecution always lingered over. Both Evelyn Gamble and Rae Boyd, Pearl's two friends who had gone with her to the dance, gave their version of events in the hushed courtroom. It was Rae who was clear about McGladdery's light-blue suit and red tie, but it was also Rae who seemed to remember a car passing them at a corner on the road just after they left Pearl at the crossroads.

The defence were quick to tear apart this statement which had come almost out of the blue. The two males with the girls in the car that night, Billy Morton and Derek Shanks, did not remember any car, although they admitted that they could have been mistaken. James Brown would have felt that with Rae Boyd's revelation he had scored a point with the jury, as it introduced an element of doubt amid the overwhelming certainty of the previous witnesses.

At the end of that day, when the shortie overcoat and tie which had been recovered from the septic tank were submitted to the court as evidence, Brian Maginess had to tell the jury that, although the stains on these items were suggestive of blood, he could not positively identify them as being caused by blood. It may have seemed an important point, and today it would be crucial, but back then there was no particular test the forensic scientists could perform to clarify the matter. The circumstances surrounding the secretion of the items was enough to suggest the stains were from Pearl's blood.

Surprisingly, the next day, 11 October, Maud Wilson made an appearance at the court and was shown into the witness box. Despite her nervous disposition she told the court that she was positive that McGladdery had left the dance around 1.40am, and just before Edith Henning and her boyfriend William Quinn. She remembered that when he left he had an overcoat draped over his arm and that he had been wearing a light-coloured suit. She was specific about the fact that she had not seen any marks on McGladdery's face that night but had noticed definite scratches under his right eye when he returned some days later to the Orange Hall accompanied by the police.

The day continued with witness after witness taking the oath, each one piecing together the events of that January night for the jury as he or she remembered them. Two very convincing young women, Heather Kennedy and Patricia Morrow, who were both employed as linen designers and had a keen eye for fashion, and in particular colour, were adamant that at the dance McGladdery's suit had been light blue and unmistakably so, even under artificial light.

To shore up the timings in relation to the accused leaving the dance after 1.30am but no later than 1.45, Edith Henning and William Quinn were called next. Both had placed the time they left the dance at round 1.35, a full five minutes before Maud Wilson had said, which, if McGladdery had gone before they had, meant that he had left around 1.30.

The defence had little to take issue with, other than to suggest that these two witnesses had got the time wrong, or to imply that Wilson had been wrong about their client leaving before Henning and Quinn. It was very difficult for Brown to stem the flow of the prosecution's 'circumstantial' case. Each witness seemed to underpin the previous witness's testimony, and any rebuttals were weak, even desperate.

He was struggling with cross-examinations. Part-time band musician and salesman Kenneth Cowan was pressed by Brown as to the song which McGladdery had allegedly asked him to play on the night of the dance. He suggested to Cowan that McGladdery had actually asked for another title, which Cowan was unable to play. Brown put it to the witness that his client had actually asked for the title 'The French Foreign Legion', but when he could not get that played, he settled for a very popular tune of the time, 'It's Now or Never'. Cowan was adamant that this was not the case and firmly stood his ground, also reaffirming that McGladdery had been wearing a light-blue suit on that night.

The only probable reason Brown may have had for troubling with any cross-examination at all was to try to diffuse the mental image the jury may have formed of McGladdery standing watching from the side of the hall as this tune was played. The title and the lyrics of the song in the context of the events that followed were enough to send a chill through the courtroom. Even though it was purely circumstantial evidence, and had no merit other than to suggest the defendant's intentions towards Pearl, it was still damaging.

As Day Three drew to a close James Brown consulted with his client about the coming hours in court, and how he intended to try to tip things in their favour. He knew Special Constable Hugh Crawford was about to take the stand, and given what McGladdery had told him about the man's behaviour after he had waded across the river on 29 January, he believed it would impact upon the jurors.

The ever-sensational trial went into Day Four with Special Constable Crawford being accused of less than professional behaviour by Brown. The barrister suggested to Crawford that on the day after Pearl's body had been found, and McGladdery had tried to shake off his 'tail' by wading through the river, the police officer had put his client in fear of his life. Raising his voice to emphasise the point, he said, 'Would it be right that you drew your gun, pointed it at McGladdery and told him to get into the car or you would put a bullet in him?'

It was a startling accusation, and one which the witness denied emphatically. What Brown went on to suggest was that Crawford had then taken McGladdery back to Newry Police Station, where he remained for eight hours, until 11 that night, under continuous interrogation by at least eight different police officers. All that Crawford could offer was that he had taken McGladdery there until his clothes had dried out, and that the defendant had gone there willingly. For Brown this was only the starting point. Judge Curran showed his discomfort at the unauthorised detention of the accused at the police station, if indeed that were the case, but he was in no way convinced that Crawford had produced a gun and threatened McGladdery.

With the appearance in the witness box of Head Constable McComish, Brown now started to question the terms McGladdery was said to have used in the various conversations and interviews which had taken place with the police. Brown was now suggesting that his client had only ever mentioned that he may have been able to produce the overcoat, but had never mentioned anything about a suit. In fact, he said, his client would never have referred to another suit because he had never owned a light-coloured suit.

When Dr Paddy Ward gave his evidence, the prosecution homed in on the injuries to McGladdery's face and hands, asking the GP for his opinion as to how the defendant's explanation for those injuries fitted alongside his own examination of McGladdery on 28 January.

The cuts to the defendant's hands were, in the doctor's opinion, consistent with his having used a file by holding the rough end in his grip while pushing or forcing the tang through or into something. In addition he did not believe the marks under McGladdery's right eye had been caused by an accident with the chest expanders.

Because McGladdery had been known to carry out shoe repairs at his house and would have used a variety of tools with which to do so, it was not difficult for Brown to counter the implication about the marks on his client's hands. But the cuts under his right eye were harder to explain.

Matters moved on, and with Agnes McGladdery now about to be called to the stand, Brian Maginess made an application to the judge to treat her as a hostile witness, bearing in mind that she had changed her story from the original comments made in front of police at her house the afternoon Robert McGladdery was first questioned. For whatever reason, Judge Curran denied the application.

When Agnes McGladdery took her place in the witness box and read aloud the oath, she must have felt the weight of the stares from the public gallery and in particular the 12 men scrutinising her from across the room. It would have been difficult for her to retract her statement that when she had spoken to her son on the morning of 28 January he had said that he had seen Pearl go home in a car with two men. However, when pressed by Maginess, she replied, 'I might have been a bit mixed up.'

She told the court that she may have been told how Pearl got home during a conversation she had with a Mrs Weir on her way back to the house after work. She was being vague. There was no corroboration from any Mrs Weir, and neither would there be. The Crown must have concluded that Agnes McGladdery's testimony was unconvincing and decided there was nothing to be gained by pressuring the old woman. There was also the fact that one of their next witnesses could be their most impressive.

The figure sitting in the dock remained almost detached from the proceedings going on around him, and even when his drinking buddy Will Copeland was called to give evidence, he barely raised an eyebrow. The story Copeland relied upon was the one he had told the police previously. There was no variation. He had seen McGladdery change from his dark suit into his light-blue suit at the house, and put on a pair of leather shoes which he had polished in front of him. The overcoat McGladdery had taken on their night out was the fawn-coloured shortie. And it was inside this coat that the two files which he had purchased during the afternoon remained. As far as the chest expanders were concerned, McGladdery had shown him how they worked, but he had not had an accident with them, and he had had no marks on his face that evening.

Whatever slant Brown or O'Donnell put on it, Copeland appeared solid, but they had plans to totally refute his evidence. They started by suggesting to Detective Sergeant Samuel Jeffrey during his spell in the box that what McGladdery had actually said to him in relation to the missing evidence was in fact, 'Give me 24 hours and I might be able to tell you who had the shortie fawn overcoat.'

It was clear that the defence were attempting to implicate someone else in the murder, and show that McGladdery's persistent refusal to tell the police where the clothes were was because he was protecting that someone. That someone was, of course, Will Copeland.

Another attempt to pour more uncertainty over the professionalism of the police was made when Brown insisted that Detective Sergeant Charles Hunter should have made McGladdery sign his notebook after he supposedly made notes relating to their conversation at Damolly on 10 February. The conversation had allegedly consisted of Robert telling Hunter that if they hadn't got the clothes the night before then they would never get them. Brown insisted Hunter admit that the statement was 'significant', and if that were the case, then why had he not done as was expected of a police officer of his experience and knowledge: read over the statement to McGladdery and have him sign the notebook agreeing to the content. It challenged the very admissibility of the evidence, given that he further suggested that the whole conversation was carried out without his client being cautioned.

There is no telling if the jury were overly concerned with the technicalities, and there were a few. What they did sit up and take notice of, though, was the evidence of Dr Marshall, the state pathologist, as he gave them a blow-by-blow account of how he thought the murder had happened in relation to the physical findings of the victim's injuries. He described a horrific series of events, made all the worse because the attack would have been prolonged and relentless. Diagrams of the shape of the stab wounds on Pearl's body helped to narrow down the type of weapon used during the attack and to show consistency between the files McGladdery was known to have purchased and those wounds. Those in the courtroom who had not known exactly how Pearl had met her end were now in no doubt that the killer had been unusually cruel.

The prosecution's case was now complete, and although little seeds of doubt had been planted along the way by the defence, these would find it difficult to gain any purchase. The damage was already done.

The only significant aspect to the defence case when it opened was the calling of McGladdery himself to give evidence. Finally the court was to hear from the man himself, the only person who knew exactly where he was and what he was doing on the night Pearl Gamble went missing. As might have been expected from a man fighting for his life, his story contradicted every one of the prosecution witnesses' versions of events. He stated categorically that he had never been to Pearl's house and did not know where she lived, and that he had never owned a light-blue suit.

According to McGladdery, he and Will Copeland had gone to the dance after a few drinks in the town, but it was Copeland who had been wearing leather shoes and a red-and-black tie which he had borrowed from McGladdery. And it was Copeland who had been carrying an extra herringbone overcoat and an extra pair of shoes in the pockets of that coat, all of which he had deposited in the cloakroom beside McGladdery's own fawn shortie. When, at the end of the dance, McGladdery found himself on his own, he had gone to retrieve the shortie overcoat but it, along with the shoes and the herringbone overcoat, were gone. In their place was the second herringbone overcoat, which he took home, assuming his friend had taken the rest of the clothing when he had left earlier.

The story was not only elaborate, but surprisingly poorly thought out. What was clear about it, though, was that it was intended to point the finger at Will Copeland as the murderer, with McGladdery the hapless patsy.

The defendant's account was riddled with holes. There were too many witnesses who had seen Copeland in the early hours of the morning, directly after the dance. He simply would have had no opportunity to make his way up to the Upper Damolly crossroads any time over that period or after. It was an absolutely absurd concoction.

Nevertheless, the story was further played out as McGladdery stated that he had not told the police about the whereabouts of the coat because he had wanted to consult with his friend Copeland.

The picture he was painting of himself was of a man who had been persecuted by the police simply because of his 'reputation' and his continual refusal to 'rat' on his friend. His barrister then quizzed him as to the extent of the surveillance the police had carried out on him and how this had affected him. It probably wasn't much of an exaggeration, but even if it wasn't, McGladdery didn't display much emotion when he replied, 'A few people would start to follow … more would join in and the crowd would get bigger and bigger until there were hundreds following us. I suppose you could call it a procession.'

If anything, McGladdery had been struck by his own infamy, and this was a boast rather than the words of a man harassed. Finally Brown asked his client directly if he had murdered Pearl Gamble. The answer he got was an emphatic 'No'.

After a brief recession for lunch the Attorney General began his cross-examination of the accused. There was little chance of McGladdery now changing any part of his story, but there were opportunities for Maginess to undermine every part of it. One of the simpler questions he asked was why, when McGladdery had noticed that his coat had been taken at the end of the dance, did he not think to inform Maud Wilson or her husband? Again McGladdery said that he had assumed his friend Will Copeland had taken it by mistake.

For some bizarre reason Judge Curran allowed a break in the cross-examination when it was intimated by McGladdery that possibly he could make further efforts to find the missing clothes. It was now Saturday, 14 October, and Curran decided to adjourn the court until Monday in order to establish whether there was any substance to McGladdery's statement, and to afford him the opportunity to consult with his counsel if there was. The missing light-blue suit being produced at this stage, even during the latter stages of the trial, would prove significant to either the defence or the prosecution.

On Monday McGladdery could offer no further information, and the closing statements began.

One particular witness who came to the attention of the prosecution team during the trial but was never called upon to give evidence still had his statement recorded. An inmate himself at Armagh jail, Patrick Joseph McKenna requested the presence of a police officer so that he could impart a revelation regarding an alleged conversation on 4 October between him, Herbert Mullan and Robert McGladdery when they had all been sharing a cell in Crumlin Road. A detective sergeant recorded the statement on 15 October and it was given directly to Maginess to consider what merit it held, if any, and whether he and his team would consider calling McKenna as a material witness. Even though the content of the alleged conversation, should it have been made known to the jury, could have been damning for McGladdery, the strength of the prosecution's case overall was substantial and the introduction of a 'new' witness may only have served to muddy the waters rather than lend any credibility. I suspect that the testimony of a convicted felon would have been subject to extreme cross-examination from the defence, and given the fact that the prosecution knew very little if anything about McKenna's motives, he may have proved to be more of use to O'Donnell and Brown than to Maginess and his team.

According to McKenna, the topic of the conversation the three cellmates had was originally about cars, Mullan having a keen interest in them, and this prompted McGladdery to remark, 'It's a pity I did not know yous two outside.' He went on to suggest that they could have helped him out of a spot by saying that they had actually given him a lift home on the night of the dance, dropping him off by car at his front door. This plan was immediately scuppered by Mullan, who said that unfortunately he did not have a car at that time. It was McKenna, though, who then suggested that he and Mullan could have been returning from Belfast on a motorbike in the early hours, and with a little bit of imagination the three came up with the rest of the story. They agreed that as they had entered Newry the bike had seized somewhere on the Belfast Road close to Damolly Road, and while waiting for the bike to cool down, both Mullan and McKenna had witnessed a man in a fawn-coloured overcoat walk up the main road and into Damolly Lane. After about ten minutes or so they also saw a cyclist coming from the same direction and following on after the walking man. The plan was also to include the two continuing on into Newry town a short time later and remembering the time on the town clock as being 2.40am.

It was clear, if McKenna was to be believed, that should the two men get off the charges for which they were being held, then and only then could they be of any use to McGladdery. As for how they intended to approach anyone with this new information became clear when McGladdery insisted that on their release they wait until an article appeared in the newspaper referring to a motorcycle at Damolly Lane on the night of the Pearl Gamble murder.

This part of the alleged conversation appears credible, in that the hatching of such an elaborate plan is something which fits nicely with McGladdery and his scheming. It is obvious that at the eleventh hour he intended to have a miraculous recollection of a broken-down motorcycle at the junction of the Belfast Road with Damolly Lane and call upon Luke Curran to make an appeal for its owner or rider to come forward and corroborate his story about walking home.

There would have been gaping holes in this story, of course, and Mullan and McKenna's complicity in attempting to pervert the course of justice especially during a prominent murder trial may have been just enough to deter them from going through with it. They need not have worried in that respect, as they were both handed down custodial sentences before McGladdery's trial, rendering the plan useless. What it did suggest to all that were privy to the statement and considered it plausible was that McGladdery was clearly panicking and, like a rat that was cornered, he was prepared to go to any lengths to escape the inevitable.

In summing up, Brian Maginess took approximately 80 minutes to revisit the murder and emphasise to the 12 men of the jury the crucial points of the prosecution's case, and there were many. By now the jurors were familiar with the events, and the thought of adjourning to consider the fate of the accused, although a heavy burden, was something they were ready to do. But closing statements by the defence, the prosecution and the trial judge often helped to clarify points and clear away any ambiguities. They would have to sit for just a little while longer.

As far as Maginess was concerned, there was no mistake. He faced the jury box, looked each man in the eye, imploring them that if they believed 'that the man in the dock on that awful morning of 28 January killed that young girl in this ghoulish fashion, then as men and citizens, helping in the administration of justice, and satisfied beyond all reasonable doubt, you will do your duty and bring in a verdict of guilty'.

In answer, James Brown began to pick through the points he had so stubbornly referred to throughout the trial, all the time emphasising the circumstantial aspect of the Crown's case. It took him around 100 minutes before he finally underlined the importance of fair deliberation and asked the jurors to 'weigh well all these grave matters, and arrive at a proper verdict of not guilty'.

Brown then felt it necessary to refer to the nature of the crime itself and the extreme violence rained upon Pearl, posing the question that if everything said about his client was true, 'What kind of a monster must he be? Did he look like a monster in the witness box?'

Was McGladdery actually guilty of this horrific murder?

It was around 4pm when Judge Curran began summing up, and although conscious of the extended periods all, including the jury, had had to sit through already, he took around two hours to address all the issues that had arisen during the trial. His job as trial judge was to bring clarity to certain matters raised by both defence and prosecution, and to assist the jurors with points of law. He was also to give a balanced and non-partisan appraisal of the evidence, and direct the jury to return a guilty or innocent verdict based solely on the evidence which they had heard in court, and not read in the press beforehand.

Shortly after 6pm the jury retired for deliberation. Just 40 minutes later the court was once again assembled as the jury filed back to their allotted positions and the foreman read out a verdict of 'Guilty'.

There was no whooping or wailing from the public gallery. The news was met with dignity and restraint. Even the brash young man in the dock did not seem particularly surprised or outraged. When Judge Curran went through the formalities and asked McGladdery if he had anything to say, he stood and looked around him before he spoke. 'Well, my Lord, there is a whole lot of things I could say, but I don't think it would make much difference. I quite realise your Lordship has a duty to perform to the State, but one thing I can say, there is not a man in this court can say I killed Pearl Gamble, because I didn't. I am innocent of the crime, that is all I have to say.'

There was obvious urgency attached to addressing the

various aspects of the case in consideration of the appeal lodged by McGladdery's legal team, which had been prepared beforehand in anticipation of a verdict of 'guilty'. On 17 October, the day after the verdict had been returned, the Inspector General's office requested a full report from the RUC's County Inspector of Down covering the case in full. The report, which was returned by 24 October, was certainly comprehensive, providing detailed accounts of the murder, the trial and all the background information on both Pearl Gamble and Robert McGladdery, everything in fact that was necessary for the Inspector General to make an informed recommendation. Once he had read and considered it in full, it was forwarded to the Office of the Minister of Home Affairs, with a final page which was unequivocal in its opinion:

'I consider this to be the worst case of murder in Northern Ireland for many years, and I cannot find one redeeming feature which should induce the least sympathy towards McGladdery.

'The verdict has been received with satisfaction in the Newry area and indeed throughout the country, and it is generally felt that justice has been done. No sympathy exists for McGladdery in his present unhappy position.

'While taking the most humane view possible, in the circumstances, of the case and with full knowledge of the attitude of a section of the public opinion towards capital punishment and of the difference in the law of Great Britain, I am unable to discover anything which would justify me in recommending a deviation from the due execution of the sentence pronounced upon McGladdery.

'Therefore, I recommend that the law should take its course.'

The 'difference in the law' to which he was referring was the 1957 Homicide Act (see Chapter Eight), which, of course, did not apply in Northern Ireland. It was one more avenue closed to McGladdery.

The very basis of the appeal lodged by the defence team centred mainly on the trial judge, Lord Justice Curran, and the manner in which he conducted the trial. The first point they made was that the judge had complained to the jury about how the police were being portrayed by both the accused and his counsel. Adding to this, they pointed out that the judge had continued to defend the police investigation team by stating that in order to undermine their (the police's) behaviour during the course of the whole investigation, the defence would have to produce some very strong evidence.

Virtually every point they outlined concerned the way Lord Justice Curran had addressed the jury and how they believed he had led them in no uncertain terms.

It is certainly true that Judge Curran had pointed out to the jury certain aspects of the case which he believed were poignant and necessary for them to arrive at a fair and balanced conclusion. For instance, he had insisted that, should the jury not believe the evidence of Detective Sergeant George Gibson, which had been called into question by the defence team, they should ask for his resignation from the police. The evidence Gibson gave was crucial in the sense that he had been one of the officers who had called with McGladdery at his home on the afternoon of 28 January, and had witnessed Agnes McGladdery say that Robert McGladdery had told her that he had seen Pearl go home in a car with two boys the previous evening. This was a devastating piece of evidence which served to totally contradict McGladdery's version of events, and reason enough for the defence to cross-examine and attempt to undermine Gibson on the stand.

There had possibly been some frustration on the part of Justice Curran at the defence, the mainstay of whose case lay in discrediting the police and suggesting that they had fitted the evidence around McGladdery because he was a convenient suspect.

All that Judge Curran was doing in fact was pointing out that if the jury actually believed what the defence were suggesting, they should not hesitate to recommend that the officers involved be disciplined. What he also succeeded in doing, though, was to emphasise how ridiculous this suggestion was to anyone with a modicum of sense.

The appeal grounds continued with further attacks on Curran, right down to his interruption of the defence as they delivered their closing address to the jury, ruling that no evidence had been submitted which would have proved that the accused could have witnessed George Dempsey driving the car outside the Orange Hall.

There were further accusations that Curran had 'not dealt adequately' with salient points such as the fact that there was a bridge spanning the Clanrye River close to Damolly, and that there were, in the opinion of the defence, clear inconsistencies in the evidence of Constables Keown and Thom compared with that of Allen Brooks, a defence witness who claimed to have seen McGladdery on the road in the early hours of 10 February 1961.

In addition there were a number of points which Brown referred to as being left ambiguous by Curran:

A. That Brown considered it 'difficult if not impossible' for McGladdery to have carried Pearl's body from the stubble field to Weir's Rocks without leaving a prominent trail.

B. That McGladdery's evidence to the Court was consistent with the statement he provided to the police on 28 January, and later again to Head Constable Farrelly on 1 February.

C. That his client had suffered as a result of police surveillance and the interest of the general public.

D. That he believed it was understandable that McGladdery was reluctant to lead police to the clothes which may have placed another person in jeopardy by doing so.

E. That the accused had no motive.

F. That there were no incriminating marks/materials found at McGladdery's home or on him, or nothing evidential recovered from underneath the fingernails of the deceased.

G. That when Dr Ward had examined McGladdery on the evening of 28 January, he was neither tired nor nervous.

The last issue Brown insisted on including was that Judge Curran had 'confused' the jury by inviting them to first consider possibilities and then probabilities before arriving at a true state of facts.

All in all, the defence had raised 24 points in favour of the appellant, not one of which was successful. In Lord MacDermott's opinion, and that of the other appeal judges, Lord Justice Black and Mr Justice McVeigh, Lord Justice Curran had carried out all of his duties throughout the trial without fault, neither leading, misleading or confusing the jury.

The issues they outlined as reason for the appeal were little more than a smokescreen, a toothless attack on a fairly conducted trial during which the evidence presented to the jury was open to one and only one interpretation. Certainly many of the pieces of evidence may have been circumstantial, but they all fitted the picture of a guilty man standing in the dock. The police investigation team may have made a few mistakes throughout the weeks leading up to the arrest of McGladdery, and quite rightly would have been criticised for those, but in terms of procedure and their skills as investigators, in piecing together the real truth about what happened that night they were beyond reproach. All the appeal achieved was to delay the inevitable.

CHAPTER EIGHT

WAITING FOR GOD

Although Robert McGladdery was no stranger to prison regimes, having had spells in both borstal and later in the adult system, this time around it was going to be different. His appeal having failed and his sentence having been upheld, he was not going back to the Crumlin Road to be placed among the general population. On his return there he would take up residence in the last double cell in C Wing, on the ground floor, or 'the ones' as it was known. It was the only double cell in the prison that didn't have inmates rushing to take advantage of a little bit of extra space, for he was going to the condemned cell.

Crumlin Road Prison is an A-listed (equal to mainland Britain's Grade I) Victorian construction, designed by a prominent architect of the time, Sir Charles Lanyon. Construction at the site on the Crumlin Road began in 1843 and the jail was completed and open for business two years later. It was modelled on Pentonville Prison in London, very much in keeping with the theory of a 'panoptican', a revolutionary concept in prison design introduced by the leading British legal reformer Jeremy Bentham. The original 'panoptican' design consisted of a central hall, which had vantage points from where the keepers could keep watch on the radiating wings that led from the area. The intention was to afford the inmates little if any privacy and instil in them a deep sense of uncertainty as a result of being kept under constant surveillance.

The jail had changed very little from its first days in 1845 to when Robert McGladdery walked through the main gate and down into base reception as a sentenced prisoner. The facade which faced Crumlin Road Courthouse across the street was much the same as that building, sombre, grey and forbidding, often filling inmates and visitors alike with fear and dread of what lay within. There were four wings in the jail, A Wing, forming, as it were, the most westerly ray of the sun, emanating from the central area, through to D Wing at the point farthest east. At different periods during the jail's history, right up to the time when it was closed in 1996, the type of prisoner held in each wing had varied.

Generally, though, sentenced prisoners were always housed in D Wing, with the remaining three wings occupied by a mixture of prisoners on remand, awaiting trial or held under the internment measures introduced several times in the 20th century.

On McGladdery's previous stays at Crumlin Road he would have been well aware of the condemned cell, and of the execution cell which he knew to be close by. But there had only been one execution in Belfast during his lifetime, and that was back in 1942, when he was seven and probably ignorant of its significance. But it was made all too real for him during his wait in prison for his trial date, when on 25 July, Samuel McLaughlin was executed by the hangman's noose for the murder of his wife Nellie at Cloughmills in County Antrim.

The atmosphere inside the prison when the execution took place must have been sombre, particularly as a large petition, which had been submitted in McLaughlin's defence in an attempt to sway the authorities into granting him a reprieve, had failed. Despite further appeals on his behalf, his death sentence was carried out in accordance with the warrant. For McGladdery the reality of what could happen to him if he too were convicted must have been beginning to sink in. He was no man of the people; rather he had a whole community baying for his blood. There would be very few names on any petition raised on his behalf, no public outcry should he be convicted. He would have to face his fate virtually alone.

The history of executions at Crumlin Road dates back to 1854, when a young soldier named Robert O'Neill was hanged in June for the cold-blooded murder of a colleague at their barracks in the city's North Queen Street. Being the first execution at the jail, and no provision having been made for executions, a scaffold of sorts was erected outside the main building: a semi-permanent structure which may have been used again for the execution of Daniel Ward nine years later in 1863. Ward had been found guilty of murdering his friend Charles Wilgar at Shaw's Bridge in Belfast, a heinous crime which became known as the 'Ballylesson Murder'. Ward had attacked and beaten Wilgar with a blunt instrument, which was recovered almost immediately after the body was discovered. The evidence was overwhelming, and in April of that year Ward went to meet his maker at the hand of the executioner.

The next to make the short walk to his end on the scaffold was John Daly, a hard drinker with a history of domestic violence, who attacked and killed his wife's aunt, Margaret Whitley, after a drunken argument in 1876. It appears that Daly was hanged at another location in the prison, possibly at the rear of A Wing, on another purpose-built platform. Domestic violence was the background to the next crime for which a man was hanged: a murder committed by Arthur McKeown in 1888. The killing was dubbed the 'Robert Street' murder and McKeown's victim, Mary Jane Phillips, was avenged by the hangman in January 1889, this time at the end of D Wing. McKeown's executioner, James Berry, was a bit of a celebrity of the day and was courted by the local press. In one interview he remarked that the scaffold was of a superior quality; praise indeed from a perfectionist such as Berry, who made no apologies for taking pride in his work and boasted of having 'pushed off' over 100 people.

In August 1894 a 21-year-old man by the name of John Gilmore faced the same fate as McKeown on the same scaffold, for the murder of Lyle Gardner, an elderly farmer from just outside Ballymoney in County Antrim. A relationship had developed between Gilmore and Gardner's daughter, the product of which was a child. There appeared to be some issue concerning monies being paid by Gilmore for the child's upkeep, and he and Lyle Gardner argued to a point where Gilmore decided to take the matter a stage further and shot the farmer as he sat beside the fire in his home. According to reports, Gilmore faced his death with great dignity, expressing regret for his actions and seeking God's mercy on his soul.

With the dawning of a new century came the

installation of a permanent and purpose-built condemned cell and execution room. I suspect that the semi-permanent arrangement for a scaffold, which in fairness had been effective until this point, was no longer viable in terms of expense, and if there were going to be any more hangings it was thought better to adapt a space that already existed.

At the bottom of C Wing a small staircase in the middle of the floor led down to a block of four punishment cells, which, when the authorities thought about it, could be restructured to allow room for a 'drop' room. The cell directly above that could then be turned into an execution room, and to further define the space, the two cells before that room on 'the ones' could be used as the condemned cell. The renovations were completed in 1900, and the first unfortunate to avail himself of the new facilities a year later in 1901 was a peddler called William Woods. In his case it was a question of when and not why he would eventually face the noose. Woods was an extremely violent individual who had a history of assault and in one case even manslaughter, although when one is made aware of the circumstances of the 'manslaughter' charge, it seems cold-blooded murder would have been a more fitting description. In fact, Woods had been out of prison for just a year, after serving ten years for that offence, when he carried out his next murder. On his many travels around the country he managed to endear himself to a few women in each area so that he would have a place to lay his head when passing through. At Bushmills, on the Antrim coast, Bridget McGivern had opened up her home to Woods, who had taken advantage not only of her hospitality but of her body as well. One September night the little cabin she lived in with her two small children became a bloody murder scene after Woods cut her throat from ear to ear.

The murderer showed clear signs of insanity, an underlying predilection for violence coupled with alcohol abuse, but neither was considered to mitigate the severity of the attack on Bridget McGivern. And so on 11 January 1901 William Woods made the short walk from cell to execution room and became the first person to be hanged at Crumlin Road in the new century.

It would be another eight years before the condemned cell would welcome its new occupant and the executioner's services would again be required. It is difficult for any parent to come to terms with the loss of a child, whether through accident or natural causes, but even more so if that child should die in violent circumstances. We believe that we as human beings are programmed to have strong maternal or paternal instincts which drive us to protect our offspring at all costs, and it goes against the grain when either a mother or father abuses their child or worse. When Richard

Justin was hanged at Crumlin Road in 1909 for beating his own daughter, Annie Thompson, to death with an iron bar, few tears were shed for his passing. The coroner at the time found it to be one of the worst assaults he had seen in his career, with hardly a bone left unbroken in the child's body. The execution was carried out on 12 March of that year, justice took its course and the normal order of things returned.

As Britain and Ireland began to enjoy the Roaring Twenties, a welcome relief from the restrictions of the years immediately following the First World War, a chilling reminder of the darker side of humanity came in 1922 in the form of an ex-soldier named Simon McGeown. An innocent seven-year-old girl, Maggie Fullerton, was abducted and molested by McGeown, who then murdered her and dumped her body on the Shaftsbury estate in County Antrim. A community sickened by this heinous crime was once again united in agreement when vengeance was meted out as the noose was slipped around McGeown's neck, the trapdoor opened and he fell to his death.

Just two years later, in March 1924, as Nelson Leech was making up wages at Purdy and Millard, stonemasons, a group of men burst into the office in an attempt to rob him and the rest of the staff. He ran to raise the alarm, but in doing so was shot and fatally wounded. A policeman on duty heard the shot and gave chase to one of the gang, only to be confronted himself by another of them waving a gun. A struggle ensued, the gun misfired and Constable Morteshed managed to arrest Michael Pratley.

It was an open-and-shut case. The murder weapon was in Pratley's possession, and he had been caught red-handed. The trial was short and little was offered in his defence, 8 May of that year being the date set for his execution.

Like Pratley, the only motivation William Smiley had for committing murder was his own greed. In 1928, in a farmhouse just outside the quiet County Antrim village of Armoy, sisters Maggie and Sarah McAuley were shot to death, and a sum of £40 was taken from the house. In those days it was a large amount of money, and the sisters were known to be wealthy. In fact, Smiley had worked as a farmhand for them and was only one of their many employees. When another of their staff, Kate Murdoch, found the two women lying dead in the house, having been blasted with a shotgun, it was Smiley who was dispatched to raise the alarm with the local police in Armoy. Immediately, as would generally have been the case, all the employees were considered as possible suspects, and it was only when Smiley was found to have concealed £30 inside his boot that he became the prime suspect.

Despite his continual denials after conviction, he was

hanged at eight o'clock on the morning of 8 August 1928, a day described as 'glorious', with the sun shining and Smiley, now resigned to his fate after having found his saviour in Christ some weeks before, showing no fear.

Two years later Samuel Cushnan, another farm labourer, hatched a plan to rob and kill a local postman whom he knew carried around £60 of pension money each Thursday on his route near Crosskeys in Toomebridge, County Antrim. His unsuspecting victim, James McCann, was invited to stop his bicycle at a spot Cushnan had already earmarked in advance for his ambush, on the promise of a drink of poteen. It was a fatal mistake for McCann. As McCann tipped the bottle to his lips, Cushnan reached into the hedge and pulled out a single-barrel shotgun and gunned him down. Although there were no witnesses to the actual murder, Cushnan was spotted several times as he tried to make his escape through drains and gullies, and there were other pieces of evidence recovered by the police which tied him to the scene of the crime. The Crown's case against him was mostly circumstantial but strong enough to sway a jury to convict him. The Thirties had arrived, but Cushnan would never see out the first year of the decade, as he now had a prior engagement to meet his maker on 8 April 1930.

During the Thirties the executioner was a fairly

regular visitor to Crumlin Road, carrying out his duty three more times over the next nine years. The first of those three clients was Thomas Dornan, a turf-cutter from near Ballymena. The background to Dornan's murderous rage, which led to the slaying of Bella and Maggie Aiken, lay in another domestic situation which went terribly wrong. Although married, Dornan had had an affair with Bella, the younger of the two sisters, and she had given birth to his child. The upkeep of the child was agreed by Dornan with the assistance of a local solicitor, an arrangement which stood for some time, until one day Dornan appeared as the two sisters worked side by side in a bog and he chased them with a shotgun. He shot Bella six times and Maggie four, and the whole sorry incident was witnessed by their brother James Aiken. No lengthy trial was required, no real defence offered and Dornan was hanged on 31 July 1931.

To break the mould somewhat, the next 'victim' of the hangman's noose was not a local, but in fact an American citizen. Even more bizarre, when the incident came to light, was the news that the man he had murdered was a Turkish national. A film operator from New York City, Eddie Cullens had formed a partnership with two Turkish men, Achmet Musa and Assim Redvan, to parade to the world the oldest living human being in existence, another Turk, Zara Agha, said to be

156 years old. All four men had travelled to England and had become associated with Bertram Mills's travelling circus, but it appears that all was not well within the partnership. Cullens and Musa travelled to Northern Ireland for a short stay, and during their time in Belfast and further afield entertained a few ladies along the way. Also during the visit, however, Cullens was making plans to kill his partner, and on 4 September 1931 Musa's body was found naked, save for a blue bathing cap, in a ditch near Carrickfergus, with a single gunshot wound to the head.

The blue bathing cap proved to be a key piece of evidence in the case, as one of the young ladies who had accompanied the men on an outing to Bangor during their stay had seen the cap in the glove compartment of Cullens's car and had passed comment on it.

Eventually, after an investigation which took the police all the way to Leeds in order to track down Cullens, the murder weapon was recovered and he was returned to Belfast for trial. The jury at his trial returned a unanimous verdict inside just 30 minutes, and after an unsuccessful appeal hearing on New Year's Day in 1932, Cullens was sentenced to hang. Another novelty for the jail was the visit to the condemned cell of Rabbi Shachter, the man requested by Cullens to attend to his spiritual needs as a practising Jew. A conman to the last, Cullens managed to convince the rabbi of his innocence, spurring him to make a statement to the press after the execution: 'He went to the scaffold with the deep conviction that his hands were clean and clear of the blood of this man.' It may have been easy to convince Rabbi Shachter, but there was no doubt in any one else's mind that the right man had been hanged.

When Dungannon philanderer Harold Courtney was backed into a corner by one of his lady friends and informed that he was about to become a father, he took the most drastic of actions and murdered her in cold blood. Although only 22 years old, Courtney had managed to string a few women along for some time until he eventually made up his mind and asked one of them to marry him. Unfortunately for him, though, one of the others whom he had been seeing, Portadown girl Minnie Reid, had fallen pregnant, an event which threatened all his plans. Now in a corner, Courtney lured Minnie out to Derryane, a remote rural spot just outside Portadown, where, after a struggle, he cut her throat with a razor and left her dying on the ground. Her heavily pregnant body was found about a week later by children playing in the area, and a murder hunt began. It was only a short time later that evidence led to Courtney as the prime suspect, and he was arrested and charged. After a five-day trial with over 50 witnesses giving evidence, Courtney was convicted, and was hanged on 7 April 1933. Again, as with most of the executions in Belfast, a large crowd gathered outside the jail to stand and wait for the death notice to be posted on the little wicker gate leading out of the main entrance. The mood of the crowd was described as sombre, and Courtney's departure from this world was reported as being dignified. But the crowds who had turned up that morning were not just thrill-seekers: many were protesters who had very serious objections to the retention of the death penalty in murder cases, and their numbers were swelling. Whether that was the reason why it would be almost another decade before the next hanging at the jail is not clear, but when it did come, it was again not without controversy.

During the Second World War many young men and women from both north and south of the border fought shoulder to shoulder alongside the Allied forces facing Hitler's tyranny. They were united in one cause: to defend the free world against oppression and domination. In Northern Ireland, though, the IRA had seized the opportunity and continued attacks on the Crown forces, who, although already stretched, coped as well as could be expected with the enemy from within.

On 5 April 1942 a small group of IRA volunteers armed with handguns gathered together in Kashmir Street in Belfast intent on attacking a police patrol. Of the six men, none was over the age of 21, the youngest being just 19. The group had among them Thomas Williams, a ranking officer even though he had yet to see his twentieth birthday, Joseph Cahill, Harry Cordner, James Perry, John Oliver and Patrick Simpson. The six men lay in wait until, a short time later, they fired at a passing police patrol, which, although hit several times, chased the men into Cawnpore Street. All six were forced to take shelter in a house and a siege began almost immediately, the police having surrounded the property within minutes.

In the ensuing gunfight Constable Patrick Murphy was shot five times from the area of the kitchen as he tried to approach the rear of the house. There was a lot of confusion at the time, with Williams claiming some time after to have shot Constable Murphy. Both Cahill and Perry also claimed to have fired the fatal shots, but, rather than just one of the men being tried for the murder, all six faced the charge, and all six were convicted and sentenced to death by hanging in August that year. The decision made history, in Northern Ireland at least, but it was soon clear that public opinion was dead set against all six men being executed, and with a legal appeal already launched, it looked likely that Belfast Crown Court would reverse or even revise its judgement under the weight of that opinion. However, on completion of the appeal on 21 August, it upheld the conviction and sentence, and set a new date of 2 September for all six to be executed. A further appeal was launched in the form of open petitions, and after only a few days there were several thousand signatures from ordinary folk as well as clergy and politicians.

On consideration and after several meetings of government officials, a further decision was made to grant a reprieve to all but one of the six men. The only one of the group to be left to face the executioner for his part in the murder of Constable Murphy was young Tom Williams.

It must have been an untenable position for the authorities to be in, with either decision destined to be unpopular in the eyes of differing sections of the community. But, in a time of world war and civil unrest, for the killing of a policeman to have gone unpunished would have sent the wrong message to the terrorists. Someone had to pay the ultimate price for murdering a representative of the Crown if only to serve as an example to those considering a similar course of action.

In the two decades between the execution of Tom Williams and that of Samuel McLaughlin, the condemned quarters and the execution cell at Crumlin Road lay dormant, being used on occasion to store bedding and other things when space was at a premium. The resurrection of capital punishment was not a welcome one, especially as all across Ireland and mainland Britain there were numerous people campaigning vigorously for its abolition. Society as a whole was considered to have moved on in leaps and bounds from the dark, depressing days of the Victorian era, and to have entered a new and refreshing age where human rights and fair play were paramount. Many considered capital punishment barbaric, favouring extended custodial sentences. But although governments of the time were aware of the strength of opposition from the abolitionists, they were not moving at any great speed to remove what they still considered to have been a useful and effective deterrent against acts of premeditated homicide.

What did happen, however, was a significant change in English law in 1957 with the introduction of the Homicide Act, providing 'partial' defences for defendants accused of murder in common law, and abolishing the doctrine of 'constructive malice'. In simple terms, if the law can ever have simple terms, before the introduction of the Act a defendant who had caused a death during the course of committing another felony was considered as having malice aforethought, the 'mens rea' (guilty mind) required to complete the offence of capital murder. No distinction was made between the defendant who had fully intended to cause death or do grievous bodily harm while engaged in the other felony, a robbery for instance, and the defendant who had caused the death accidentally during the commission of his offence. The Homicide Act removed this link between the two separate crimes, as well as introducing the partial defences of diminished responsibility and suicide pact. Capital murder still carried the death sentence, whereas a conviction for murder almost always ended with the imposition of life imprisonment.

One of the reasons why the Act was introduced was the fallout from the famous trial and subsequent execution of Derek Bentley in January 1953. Derek Bentley, just 19, and his 16-year-old friend Christopher Craig were small-time criminals and both of limited intelligence. On 2 November 1952 they had been trying to break into a warehouse by gaining entry through the roof when they were spotted and the police alerted. One of the attending officers climbed on to the roof of the building and detained Bentley, who was then alleged to have shouted, 'Let him have it, Chris.'

Armed with a small modified revolver, Craig took a shot at Detective Sergeant Fairfax, who was still holding Bentley, hitting him in the shoulder. The wound was only superficial and Fairfax stood his ground, arresting Bentley, who had in his pocket, but never produced, a knife and a knuckle-duster. When police backup arrived and made their way on to the roof, Craig fired all his rounds, one of which struck Constable Sidney Miles in the head and killed him instantly. Cornered and with no options left, Craig jumped 30 feet to the ground and was arrested as he lay there injured.

The trial was short, covering only three days in all, but the implications from the guilty verdict, which entailed a mandatory death sentence for murder, would last for over 40 years: until 1998, when the Court of Appeal set aside Bentley's conviction.

During the trial it emerged that Craig would not face the hangman simply because of his age. Bentley, however, regardless of the fact that he did not fire the shots that wounded Fairfax and killed Miles, would face the death sentence only because the law did not have an option to charge him with manslaughter, because at the time of the killing he was involved in a felony offence which came within the description of 'constructive malice'. Even though he was actually under arrest and detained by Fairfax when Miles was fatally wounded, the court believed that he was attempting to make good his escape when Craig fired on Fairfax.

This wasn't the only contentious aspect to the case. There was inconclusive forensic evidence as to the calibre of bullet which killed Miles and whether that bullet was fired by Craig or perhaps another police officer at the scene, many of whom had been carrying weapons on the night. That and the fact that a psychiatric evaluation of Bentley, which uncovered his actual mental age as that of an 11-year-old, should and would have been enough today to return a wholly different verdict and sentence.

It was the public reaction to the case which effectively spurred debate and the eventual change to the law with the introduction of the 1957 Homicide Act. The very positive effects the Act had on cases brought before the courts from 1957 onwards were obvious, as the amount of executions carried out each year in England was reduced by 75 per cent, averaging four each year instead of around 15. The writing was on the wall and in one way or another the abolitionists were gradually winning their fight against capital punishment.

Unfortunately for Robert McGladdery, though, the Homicide Act passed into law only in mainland Britain and was not applicable in Northern Ireland.

I cannot be sure just how much interest McGladdery took in current affairs or even if he ever bothered picking up and reading a newspaper. If he had, while the police were frantically searching for the clothing he had discarded, on 6 February 1961 he would have been aware of the beginning of the trial of Samuel McLaughlin at Belfast Crown Court.

The murder of Nellie McLaughlin by her husband in October the previous year was a sad and sorry tale, made worse by the fact that it appears to have been carried out by a normally good-natured man acting in the throes of a drunken stupor. The murder occurred in Nellie's mother's house in the quiet County Antrim village of Cloughmills, and although McLaughlin was originally from Derby in England, he was a popular figure, having made many friends since relocating to Northern Ireland.

Each day of the trial was reported by the *Belfast Telegraph* and the *Newsletter*, as well as local publications in the Ballymena area. For some reason McLaughlin's plight captured the public imagination, and when he was convicted and sentenced to death, petitions from Cloughmills as well as Derby were submitted in an attempt to overturn the decision. Regardless of their efforts, McLaughlin was hanged on 25 July 1961, and one inmate in particular must have felt particularly vulnerable when, at 8am that day, the prison fell silent.

CHAPTER NINE

PLEA FOR
MERCY

When Robert McGladdery walked into the large double cell on 22 November 1961 and met the two warders charged with looking after him for the foreseeable future, the cockiness and the bravado were most probably still there. In his mind, I believe, he always thought there was a way out: this wasn't the end of Robert Andrew McGladdery, the man who could talk his way out of almost anything, the man who had led the police a merry dance for over a week. But as the reality began to sink in, and no leave was granted to appeal to the House of Lords, McGladdery took to writing a 16-page 'autobiography' to accompany a petition which was rapidly being organised for submission to Lord Wakehurst, the then Governor of Northern Ireland, in a last-ditch plea for mercy.

It is safe to say that McGladdery's legal team held out little hope that this submission would prove fruitful. Public opinion went a good way towards swaying the decision that was being considered, and John de Vere Loder, 2nd Baron Wakehurst, being an astute politician as well as a seasoned public servant – he had held the post of Governor of New South Wales from 1937 to 1946 and then the Governorship of Northern Ireland since 1952 – was going to do nothing less than serve the wishes of the people.

Until the executive committee had met, deliberated and made their final decision, all that McGladdery could do was to acclimatise to his new surroundings and make the best of a bad situation. In truth, the condemned cell offered a lot more comfort than any other in the jail, with inmate number 237/1961 also able to avail himself of a large and diverse menu. An internal document had been drafted by the prison's governor for approval by the Ministry of Home Affairs outlining the proposed breakfast, lunch and evening meals they intended to serve to the condemned inmate. Eggs, bacon and sausage at breakfast and the choice of chops, steak, fish or liver at dinner was more than McGladdery would normally have had at home. But in addition to this, he also had a daily allowance of two bottles of stout (possibly Guinness) and 20 cigarettes. If there were any pluses to occupying the large double cell at the end of C Wing, and most would agree that there weren't, perhaps it was that the inmate's last few days on this earth would be comfortable.

The only small glimmer of hope for a successful outcome to the petition hastily being circulated throughout all areas of the province had come on 11 October, while McGladdery's trial was in its earliest stages. Another prisoner who had been condemned to death and had been occupying the 'death cell' at Crumlin Road was given a last-minute reprieve by the Governor of Northern Ireland.

George Bratty, a 26-year-old from Donacloney in Armagh, had been tried and convicted in May that year of the murder of Josephine Fitzsimmons, an 18-year-old girl from Hillsborough. His appeal against conviction was considered and dismissed by the Northern Ireland Court of Appeal, but the door had been left open for a further appeal to the House of Lords. That further appeal was rejected and conviction upheld on 6 September, although a date for his execution was not set until the Lords' ruling was submitted on 3 October. The circumstances were obviously different from McGladdery's, and it was not entirely clear whether it was a question of the strength of public opinion against his death sentence being carried out or the suggestion that Bratty had committed the crime while in a state of mental impairment, but the Cabinet's decision was to recommend to the government that the sentence be commuted to life imprisonment.

Every case is different, of course, and the salient points for Lord Wakehurst to consider in McGladdery's petition were laid out in a fashion which only suggested the content but delivered very little. The first consideration, according to his legal team under James Brown, was McGladdery's age. How they could even think that would have made any difference was inconceivable. In fact, they must have considered the comparisons that the committee would have drawn between the age of the offender and the age of his victim. Pearl was, after all, only 19 when McGladdery showed her no mercy whatsoever.

Yet again the speculation and the rumours which surrounded the defendant and the case in general were pointed out as 'significant' by Brown in terms of the petition. There had been a reference made somewhere in the press to the fact that, should McGladdery be acquitted of Pearl's murder, he was still going to be rearrested and returned to mainland Britain for questioning in relation to another killing, that of Brenda Nash. That murder had taken place at some time after the 12-year-old girl had disappeared on her way back home to her parents' house in Heston in Middlesex on 28 October 1960. Her body was found dumped in a Hampshire wood over two weeks later – she had been strangled. There was absolutely no truth in this rumour of McGladdery's supposed involvement in this murder at all, but it hadn't stopped the press circulating details and commenting on the similarity of the circumstances. In fact, some months later Arthur Albert Jones confessed to the girl's murder while in jail serving four months for another assault on a female in the same area.

What Brown was attempting to highlight was the fact that he believed McGladdery had suffered at the hands of the press since the investigation had first begun, hinting that the possibility always remained that the jury at his trial could very well have been swayed, as could the opinions of the public at large. Without this negative press, he believed, his client would not have been vilified to the extent he had been, and indeed may have had much greater public sympathy.

The third point he made reference to was the difference in the law between Northern Ireland and mainland Britain in respect of the 1957 Homicide Act. There was little point in labouring this issue, as Brown well knew, but he was clutching at straws. The law of the land was just as it stated, and the appeal was for clemency only. This aspect had already been considered and dismissed.

Among the documents then there was an intriguing inclusion. McGladdery was intent on venting his spleen in his 'autobiography', which he had sat down, composed and handwritten in a wide-ruled exercise book.

When I opened the little book to read the contents I was glad that it was accompanied by a typed version, as in places the handwriting was slightly cramped and manic. I am not sure what I expected from it – possibly the purging of a troubled soul, certainly a full and frank admission of guilt – but never did I believe that for a man in such a precarious position as he was, he would not take the opportunity to present himself, albeit abstractly, as prostrate and repentant.

McGladdery starts by telling the reader about his earliest memories, and how his mother had told him about the night he was born up at Derrybeg, close to the viaduct which carried the trains over the valley and on towards Dublin and the south. He then brings us on to his first school days, when he says he was beaten with a stick for not being able to perform basic sums and spellings. These first negative experiences are what he blames for prompting his absences from class and the fact that he filled his days with his passion for hunting rabbits and walking his dog everywhere.

He describes his parents as hard-working, labouring at nearby Henning's farm and likely to still be at work when he was due to return home for his tea. The picture he paints of these early years is of a 'latchkey' kid, very much left to his own devices and fending for himself. Moving from one school to another appears to have made little difference to him, and he cut short his academic career in October 1950. From then on his only interests were playing the bagpipes and hunting with his ferret. He tries to convey an unhappy time at school, a time when most children are nurtured and shaped into healthy, well-adjusted young men and women, remembering their school days as the best time of their lives. For him, apparently it was a time of struggle and disappointment.

It is typical of McGladdery to twist the story and displace the blame, choosing to apportion it to the very people who were working such long hours to provide him with a better future. He also fails to accept that he may have contributed to his own shortcomings at school, for we already know that he was of average intelligence. Just a few lines from his little book give the impression more of a hard-luck story than an open and honest appeal from the heart.

The first incident which supposedly takes McGladdery down a wayward path happens as a result of his being assaulted by a male much older than himself. While out ferreting one afternoon, McGladdery says, a local farmer catches him in his field while his ferret is still in a burrow seeking out rabbits. This much older man assaults him and moves him on, but without letting him retrieve his ferret. He then writes about his determination to get back what is his and how he is adamant that he will do almost anything to get it back, or to take something in its place. Unable to get his ferret back, he states, he returns to the farmer's land and enters his cottage, robbing the man's wife at gunpoint with a home-made .22 pistol and taking a shotgun.

This leads to his first 'real' brush with the law, and two years in borstal, where he remembers learning his trade as a shoe mender as well as lessons in criminal behaviour from his fellow inmates. Whether there is any accuracy in his telling of this story is neither here nor there, but what it does do is highlight a common thread running through the whole document. McGladdery consistently tells the reader that his behaviour was always a consequence of others' attitudes towards him. It is as if he believes he can justify his actions by showing just how much of a victim he was himself. If there are elements of truth in the story of the farmer, what it also highlights, of course, is the lack of proportionality in his response to being treated as he was by the man. There could not have been any justification for robbing the farmer's wife at gunpoint, certainly not because of her husband's alleged behaviour towards McGladdery for trespassing. Most young men would have accepted a clip around the ear as fair treatment for such a transgression, but not McGladdery. At a very early stage in his life he has shown that violence is how he intends to deal with most situations where he either wants something and cannot get it any other way, or where he believes he has been wronged and seeks compensation. And it doesn't seem to matter whether his victim is male or female.

As mentioned above, for this incident involving the firearm he receives a custodial sentence in borstal, a place he describes as 'offal' (awful). Generally there are few mistakes of spelling or grammar in his writing, certainly fewer than I expected, bearing in mind the age at which he had left school and his lack of interest in anything academic. One other mistake, however, which took me a while to decipher, was the word 'caffey', used when he tried to illustrate how, on his release from borstal, certain characters he knew had noticed a great change in him as a person, among those the people in the 'caffey'. He was, of course, referring to a 'cafe', a meeting place so popular among the young men and women of the time. A very competent attempt to spell the word phonetically, this suggests someone who was anything but illiterate.

The self-serving rambling then continues with McGladdery recounting an incident which occurred after his release from borstal, when he says he had decided to make a new start by taking off to England in search of employment. He has little money to get there, so he decides to take £50 from his sister, who had been saving up for her wedding. He describes how, after taking the money and then boarding the train at Newry, he is gripped by regret and guilt, and continues to wrestle with his conscience even as the train pulls out of the station. But before long he throws off his dilemma: he says that he jumps from the moving train and makes his way back towards the town and to the home of a policeman he knows as John Carroll, a 'Christian' man and a friend. After tea and a sympathetic ear he returns to his home and replaces the money, making his peace with everyone.

This is possibly one of the only attempts McGladdery makes to show that he is capable of determining right from wrong and weighing up the consequences of his actions. It is, however, an incident which is purely anecdotal, and can never be evidenced. There is an audit trail left behind in the form of McGladdery's criminal record which is rather damning and certainly more convincing than the heart-warming tale of a repentant young man.

Eventually McGladdery moves on to the period when he makes his way to the mainland and sets up first in Manchester, quickly finding employment. Almost immediately, his first day at a new job in a factory no less, he becomes involved in a dispute with another worker over a seat around the lunch table. The dispute leads to a fight, one which McGladdery says he wins convincingly. He is obviously proud of his physical capabilities. He can handle himself, and this makes him determined. His writings reveal that: 'I had learned something that day, I thought if a man was willing to fight for something he wanted, he was almost sure to get it.' If it were interpreted ordinarily, the word 'fight' would mean 'struggle' in the abstract sense, but I believe McGladdery intends the word to be taken literally here. He sees the world in simple terms: if he wants something enough, his physical strength and his ability with his fists will get him just that.

His time in Manchester is a settled period for him, and he refers to a girlfriend called Pamela. His description of their relationship is rather vague, and I suspect that it is much more physical than emotional, petering out when he eventually leaves Manchester and makes his way to Brighton. Here he finds another girlfriend, Patricia, who appears more of a long-term prospect but who quickly leaves his life when he is arrested and imprisoned for possession of a firearm which had been found hidden in his digs after a police tip-off.

McGladdery skips merrily over the incidents for which he is arrested, as if they have little if any importance to the story in general. He makes no attempt to explain the circumstances surrounding them, choosing rather to dwell on his time in various institutions, and how these incarcerations and the treatment he receives during them only serve to accelerate his destructive behaviour.

One of the most disturbing incidents he refers to is at

Pentonville Prison in London, where, for assaulting a warder, he is tied to a wooden exercise horse and given 12 strokes with the birch as punishment. According to him, he is constantly haunted by this image and has recurring dreams about the episode. He describes this type of punishment as barbaric and fit only for an animal, yet it does little to deter him from doing exactly the same thing again. There are yet more assaults on prison staff at various institutions and he appears to have been constantly moved from one jail to another as a result, forfeiting remission as he went.

It is hard to understand how the submitting of this document could further a clemency appeal. One minute McGladdery was railing about his inhumane treatment at the hands of the prison authorities, the next he was enthusiastically describing his own acts of violence in glorious technicolour.

But probably the most poignant comment he makes is on his release from prison in February 1958: 'That morning I walked free. I had the idea in my head that the world owed me plenty and I wasn't going to worry too much how I got it.' What must have been foremost in every one of his readers' minds was that three years later, almost to the very week, McGladdery tried to do just that, but with dire consequences.

The frightening thing about McGladdery's writings is that there is not one single expression of remorse for what he did to Pearl Gamble. Nor is there any admission of guilt. He appears to be in total denial. To truly show remorse for one's actions, one must first take responsibility for those actions, but that is something he seems incapable of doing. According to him, he is a victim of circumstances, a man more sinned against than sinning.

On the strength of this submission alone, I believe he may have sealed his own fate.

The petition in support of McGladdery which was printed and distributed around Northern Ireland couldn't fail to have some people queuing up to put their names to it. It had been prepared by the Association for the Reform of the Law on Capital Punishment in Northern Ireland, of which Brian Garritt was the secretary. There was, of course, an element of the community intent on bringing about the abolition of the death penalty, and among those some quite influential people. But in truth, the petition sheets were often returned with only a handful of signatures on them, the numbers amounting to somewhere in the very low thousands.

The majority of the signatures were penned only a matter of days before the appointed date of execution, as in the case of Jack McClelland, representing the Ulster Vegetarian Society, whose plea for clemency was dated 13 December, only a day before Lord Wakehurst was due to submit his findings to the Prime Minister of Northern Ireland, Viscount Brookeborough. Many of the strongest objections came from clergymen and church elders of every denomination, quoting Biblical references and reminding all of the Ten Commandments, particularly 'Thou shall not kill': a double-edged sword.

The weakness in the petition was, of course, the fact that it represented a minority of the population in the North, and the strength of people's anger and resentment towards Robert McGladdery had been very vocal both in the press and out on the streets.

Another aspect to the submission was McGladdery's medical background and the possibility that he was suffering from a degree of insanity, and the defence team relied on an examination which was carried out on their behalf by Dr McCracken on 7 December. His conclusions were based on a frank and open interview with McGladdery in prison with two police officers present. Not ideal, of course, but described by McCracken as neither oppressive or restrictive. McCracken first outlines his findings, describing McGladdery in his teens and even earlier as a 'lone wolf', poorly adjusted socially, and with a suspicious attitude towards others. He touches upon the belief that aggression is what McGladdery relies on as the method by which he can acquire almost anything he desires.

When he moves towards describing McGladdery as an adult, he recognises this persecution complex continuing on from childhood and manifesting itself in the physical violence he inflicts on others. The incident of the birch plays a major part in McGladdery's hostility towards the authorities, and in Dr McCracken's opinion inspires the young man to arm himself against his aggressors.

The conclusions which Dr McCracken arrives at are heavily swayed in McGladdery's favour, as you would expect them to be, but the sympathy card he holds up in his defence relies heavily on the poor start the young man has had in life. It is a hard-luck story with little evidence of a proven medical condition. What McCracken states is that McGladdery's 'distorted' outlook categorises him as an 'aggressive psychopath' who has 'no intellectual control over his destructive emotions'.

Further to his conclusions, McCracken refers to McGladdery's stay in Norwich Prison, stating that there he underwent a number of psychiatric interviews and evaluations. In his opinion these evaluations indicated signs of mental abnormality for which there should and would have been a course of treatment were it not for the circumstances of his being incarcerated for a short period and then released back into the world with no follow-up.

Dr McCracken then refers to the electroencephalograph test which McGladdery had undertaken in Pentonville, explaining that the procedure is normally carried out when it is believed there may be a brain abnormality, but that it was also used as a specific test for epilepsy.

It had been well documented that McGladdery's father had been an epileptic, and McCracken alluded to the fact that Robert had himself suffered from the same condition, experiencing regular convulsions up until the age of seven, when those attacks miraculously disappeared.

Next he shows concerns as to McGladdery having contracted a sexually transmitted disease, not being specific in its diagnosis, only describing how it was treated with penicillin. This is interesting in the sense that McCracken does not dig any deeper into the definitive type of STD McGladdery had contracted, but chooses to skirt around it. I believe he intended to sow the seed of possibility that McGladdery had been suffering from syphilis, of which there could have been symptoms of mental impairment if this disease had reached its final stage. Tertiary syphilis, as it is called, was not common, but had been extensively documented because it had affected many well-known people throughout the ages, Van Gogh, Schubert and Al Capone among them. The case of Al Capone sticks in most people's minds, as it was when he was in prison that he displayed signs of insanity and chronic mental illness, and was diagnosed as having contracted neurosyphilis, possibly at an early age. This form of syphilis can be deeply destructive, causing damage to the nervous system, the heart, brain, joints and in extreme cases causing death.

Lastly Dr McCracken concentrates on the treatment he considers should have been appropriate to someone like McGladdery, an aggressive psychopath, which he claims involves chemicals and psychotherapy over a period of about three years.

The report alone, if accurate, could raise a degree of doubt as to McGladdery's health of mind, but if it were to be in any way corroborated, the committee would have to sit up and take notice.

It was not a coincidence that Agnes McGladdery was encouraged to pen a few paragraphs about her son. The content of her submission supported almost all the claims that Dr McCracken had made about Robert McGladdery.

The young Robert, according to her new revelations, was a deeply troubled young man who had been having treatment for epileptic episodes from birth up until his early school years. She also recalled how he had been convinced that the police were continually watching and following him, to the point where he would barricade himself and his mother into the house on some evenings. He seldom slept in his own room, choosing to sleep in with his mother on a makeshift cot, fit for someone much younger and smaller. When he did sleep in his own room, she could hear him pacing the floor and talking to himself, she said.

The picture his mother paints of him suggests the classic symptoms of someone deeply traumatised and with a severe persecution complex, paralleling the findings of Dr McCracken.

One particular incident Agnes McGladdery makes reference to is when a stray dog, which she claims Robert had befriended and took everywhere with him, was shot dead by a local farmer after it had strayed on to his land. Apparently the effect on her son was catastrophic, causing him to withdraw further into himself, so that fear and suspicion were ever more present. It is not the basis of a happy childhood or a comfortable transition into youth she describes, and if the testimony was true, one could not help but have some sympathy for Robert. But, standing in total contrast to her submission, and in many ways to Dr McCracken's, was McGladdery's 'autobiography'.

Nowhere in this document does he refer to his fits as a child, his persecution complex, or the definitive incident in his youth involving his dog. According to him, with his love of outdoor sports and his forced independence, at no time does he feel particularly vulnerable. Nor does he display any traits of being a recluse, socialising locally in bars and at dances, and even travelling on his own to England to find work.

Certainly there is anger and mistrust, but he deals with these emotions by relying on his physical presence and combative capabilities.

There was no doubt Brown was being thorough, but he had already consulted with Dr McCracken some three months earlier, and had received from him a less lengthy report which gave his opinion on McGladdery's mental state and whether he should be considering an insanity plea on his client's behalf under the McNaughton rules. These rules were the only established means by which a court could establish whether an accused was criminally insane at the time of committing an offence. They stemmed from the trial in 1843 of Daniel McNaughton, who had shot and killed Edward Drummond, the private secretary to Britain's Prime Minister at that time, Sir Robert Peel. Part-time actor and medical student, McNaughton had believed he was the victim of a conspiracy involving the Pope and the Tory government, and as a result of this delusion had shot Drummond in the back near 10 Downing Street. He was found guilty by reason of insanity and spent the rest of his life in institutions, eventually dying in Broadmoor in 1865. The benchmark statement arrived at during the case stated: 'It must be clearly proved that at the time of committing the act, the party accused was labouring under such a defect of reason, from disease of the mind, as not to know the nature and quantity of the act he was doing, or if he did know it, that he did not know what he was doing was wrong.'

By McGladdery's own admission in his 'autobiography', he knew only too well what was right and wrong. He had displayed that quite clearly when he alluded to the story about having taken his sister's wedding money only to return it later after suffering an attack of conscience. As for the issue of 'defect of reason', it is true that he had been diagnosed as having a behavioural disorder and had been deemed a psychopath, but he almost certainly knew exactly what he was doing when he had attacked Pearl Gamble. Had the assault ended with the victim walking away with a broken nose and minor injuries, McGladdery would have almost certainly ended up back in jail, and for a lengthy period, given the aggravated aspect of the offence. He knew the only way to avoid that was to make sure Pearl was never able to tell anyone who her attacker was. There was reasoning behind every action he took that night.

In answer to Dr McCracken's appraisal of McGladdery, the Minister of Home Affairs, Brian Faulkner, himself then engaged a tribunal of expert psychiatrists to examine him, their findings to be based purely on the information the condemned man would supply them. They were afforded the bonus of having a copy of McCracken's report from which to investigate the points which he had believed may have had some bearing on McGladdery's state of mind.

The tribunal consisted of Dr W. Cartan, Senior Medical Officer of the Ministry of Health and Local Government, Dr C.B. Robinson, Consultant Psychiatrist for the Northern Ireland Hospitals Authority and Resident Medical Superintendent at Purdysburn Hospital, and Dr T.W.H. Weir, Consultant for the Northern Ireland Hospitals Authority and Resident Medical Superintendent at Muckamore Abbey. The panel had no other agenda but to look at and appraise all the relevant information in a balanced and totally unbiased manner. The examination of McGladdery lasted a full two days, and took into consideration observations made by 16 members of staff at Crumlin Road, all of whom had come in contact with the prisoner since his committal on the murder charge.

The report was extensive, and made for depressing reading:

After an exhaustive enquiry we are unanimously of the following opinion.
1. There is no evidence of mental disorder now or in the past. (He was not questioned about the crime of which he is convicted and no reference was made to it by him or us.)
2. He is self-centred, egotistical, crying publicly and is of the exhibitionist type.

3. He is amoral in that he doesn't seem to have developed the rudiments of ethics, fair play or any self criticism that might guide him.

4. He is alert, has a good memory and is of at least average intelligence.

5. There is a long history of violence which he substantiated by recounting it himself without prompting by us and without shame. For example, he described an assault on a prison officer (in Norwich Prison) by butting him in the face with his head and kicking him in the face when he fell. He kicked in the stomach a prisoner who had come to the assistance of the officer.

6. In our opinion, birching did not produce any change in his character which was the same before and after. Indeed he volunteered that when he was put on bread and water for two weeks and solitary (lock-up) confinement for four weeks for violence he would have chosen birching instead. This occurred in Norwich Prison, a few weeks subsequent to the birching at Pentonville Prison.

7. He denied any knowledge of convulsions as a child and has no memory of his mother telling him of such. He believes his father died of epilepsy. With a family history of epilepsy, his mother's account of the prisoner having convulsions as a child and with Dr McCracken's reference to electroencephalographic

examination, the question of an epileptic complaint as a factor in his violence was considered carefully. There has been no evidence of major epilepsy and prison officers clearly in contact with him, especially those in the condemned cell, find no evidence remotely suggestive of blackouts, transient vagueness, or other evidence of severe epilepsy. He was under observations from the time of his arrest and under close supervision night and day from the 16th October 1961, and the absence of any such evidence of epilepsy is significant. Further the premeditation of his assaults and also clear memory of them rule out, in our opinion, epilepsy as a cause of the violence. We believe that most if not all prisoners on a Capital charge in England have an electro encephalographic examination as a routine, but while we feel that such procedure would be desirable in Northern Ireland as a regular measure, we must state that in this particular case, even the coincidence of previous epilepsy would not lead us to regard such as an explanation, much less an excuse of his violence.

8. The venereal infection referred to in Dr McCracken's report took place in August 1960 and he denies any previous infection. Such infection (which incidentally he says was gonorrhoea and not syphilis) would not be relevant to this enquiry even if

it had been syphilis because the six months between infection and the date of the crime was far too short for significant brain change and resulting psychosis.

9. The term aggressive psychopath is a succinct way of describing a type of person. It is not a clinical entity in our view.

10. McGladdery does not in our view come within the meaning of the McNaughton rules nor within the meaning of Section 2 (1) of the Homicide Act 1957.

Lord Wakehurst made his submission to the Prime Minister of Northern Ireland on 14 December, less than a week from the date for McGladdery's execution. The Executive Committee had met and, after considering all aspects of the case, had found no extenuating circumstances which would have moved them towards recommending the sentence be commuted to life imprisonment. In his submission Wakehurst included the judgement of the Court of Appeal, the petition which had been signed by several hundred people from all over Northern Ireland, McGladdery's 16-page 'autobiography' and the police report dated 2 November 1961 and addressed to the Minister of Home Affairs.

The due process of law was to be upheld and all doors had shut, and shut for good, in Robert McGladdery's face. There was to be no last-minute reprieve.

CHAPTER TEN

THE LAST FEW STEPS

I spoke recently to a retired clergyman who as a child had been evacuated from Belfast during the Second World War, and had ended up staying at Damolly Terrace with a couple with whom he came to form a lifelong friendship. Although not one of blood, their relationship was such that from those days onwards he would refer to them as his aunt and uncle. Long after the war ended he continued to spend summer holidays there with them, and his memories of that place would bring a smile to his lips. Each summer was eagerly anticipated and each visit filled with activities such as fishing in the river or exploring the surrounding fields and hills, a far cry from life in the city. In the Forties it was a home from home for the boy, a safe place far from the constant threat of Nazi bombers targeting the busy shipyards and factories in and around Belfast's docks.

As a child he was well acquainted with Robbie McGladdery, as he knew him, because his aunt and uncle's home was only a few yards away from number four and the fields opposite the houses were a huge playground for kids of all ages. His aunt had even taught at Sunday school, and McGladdery had been among those who had attended.

The customs of the country folk were different in many ways from those who lived in the towns, and the young evacuee had found them odd on more than one occasion. A good example was the time he was given a sack by his aunt and told to take it and dump it in the canal. The contents were lively in his hands as he carried it across the road and into the field, knowing full well that inside were a young cat and one of its litter of kittens. He admits to having felt guilty about what he was entrusted to do, but in those days, when it was hard enough to put food on the table at the best of times, what the household didn't need were two hungry cats and possibly more to come. He both understood and accepted why he had to do what he was told, and marched through the tall grass towards the river bank purposefully.

On his way there he encountered Robbie McGladdery, who stopped and asked what he had in the bag. When the boy explained what he was doing and opened the bag, Robbie told him that he would be happy to take the kitten but he could do what he needed with the cat. A deal was struck and he proceeded on his way to carry out the rest of his task.

When he went on to tell me that he then deposited the bag in the canal, I had my doubts, as in the next breath he said that the cat actually turned up again at the house the very next day. I suspect that he did not want to admit to having gone against his aunt's express wishes. What he did have to confess to his aunt at the time were the facts of the agreement he had made with Robbie. His aunt was anything but pleased, not just because he had not done exactly as she had asked, but because, as she told him, Robbie had often been cruel to animals, and even though her intention had been to drown the two cats, in her opinion it would have been much more humane to do so than to place them in his care.

Without hesitation his aunt marched up the street and knocked on the door of number four. When Robbie came to the door she shook her finger at him and told him in no uncertain terms that she would be keeping an eye on him, and for him to treat the kitten well, or else she would take him to task. From what the clergyman can remember of the days and months that followed, Robbie did take great care of the kitten.

It may have been just anecdotal evidence that

McGladdery had a history of mistreating animals, but I suspect there is an element of truth to it, as that particular behavioural trait fits perfectly with the definition of a true psychopath as recognised by psychiatry. It has been widely agreed that psychopaths are people who have an antisocial personality disorder, which will likely manifest itself through aggressive, perverted, amoral or criminal behaviour, and lack any remorse for their actions whatever they may be. It is also believed that, as children, psychopaths will show extreme cruelty towards pets, often torturing them and inflicting needless pain. But why then did the young McGladdery choose to treat the kitten any differently?

He may have done so out of fear of the wrath of his Sunday school teacher, for she was a strong matriarchal figure in his life. It is unlikely, though, that he felt or recognised anything about the animal's plight which would have caused him any real concern for its welfare: a lack of the ability to empathise is another well-documented trait of the psychopath or sociopath.

The Sunday school teacher, who no doubt was well aware of McGladdery's shortcomings, was a deeply committed Christian who refused to believe that there was no hope left for the young man now awaiting his fate in prison. That hope was, of course, for his eternal salvation, his soul no less, and not his mortal being. Even when her husband had tried to dissuade her from applying for visiting rights, she continued, eventually receiving permission through the post a matter of days later. It was not an easy journey to make for someone who was totally reliant on public transport. She travelled the 50 miles or so on the bus, and on getting to Belfast had to ask for directions to a part of the city she was not familiar with. This first visit to McGladdery was followed by another a few days later, and although I am not privy to the content of their conversations I can imagine that she would have tried to focus on how best she could help the young man she probably still saw as her Sunday school pupil. There was little for McGladdery to do in prison other than to contemplate his fate and the mistakes he had made over the years, but even he must have been touched by the belief she still had that, regardless of those mistakes, he still had an opportunity to turn his life around.

Her commitment to McGladdery may have moved him to ask for his old friend John Carroll, by now retired from the police, to visit him in jail, and if possible, to try to contact an evangelist whom McGladdery and Carroll had witnessed speaking some years before. It was a long shot, but with some effort it was arranged, and the preacher visited the prison just days before the date set for McGladdery's execution.

Visits to the condemned prisoner were as a rule at his request, providing the visitors were deemed appropriate by the authorities. In truth, there weren't that many over the last remaining weeks, and fewer still during the final 24 hours, his defence counsel, James Brown, and his mother Agnes being the last people to say their goodbyes on the evening of 19 December 1961.

The following morning, as light crept into the double cell in C Wing at Crumlin Road Prison, Robert McGladdery awoke from his sleep and greeted what was to be his last day on earth. According to reports, he breakfasted lightly before dressing, and was seen for a time by the Reverend William Vance, the prison's Presbyterian chaplain. The next stage in the proceedings was closely choreographed, when at a few minutes before 8am, the Under Sheriff for County Down, Wilfred Park, along with Dr Girvan and the Reverend Vance, met the prison's governor outside the execution room door on C Wing, while the executioner, Harry Allen, and his assistant stood outside the door to McGladdery's cell. As the clock struck eight Allen looked across at Park and was given the instruction to carry on.

The executioner's job was to complete the whole process as quickly and as humanely as possible, and given that Allen had over 20 years' experience there was little chance that things would not go to plan. As of 1956 he and Robert Leslie Stewart had been elevated to the role of concurrent Chief Executioners after the death of Steve Wade and the resignation of the infamous Albert Pierrepoint, and had amassed quite a body count during their appointment. A dapper man, Allen was said to wear a bow tie when attired for work or otherwise, although his manner of dress suggested eccentricity rather than a levity which would have been wholly inappropriate in his chosen career.

As soon as the executioner and his assistant entered the cell, McGladdery was made to stand and his hands were pinioned behind his back before he was led through into the little bathroom of the cell. There, he may or may not have been aware that a bookcase concealed a doorway which opened directly into the execution chamber and the workings of the gallows. He was then walked directly on to the trapdoor, where his legs were strapped, a white hood was placed over his head and a running, leather-covered noose set around his neck. When all had stood clear of the trapdoor, Allen released the lever, and McGladdery fell through the opening into the drop room. Both the executioner and his assistant then walked down the staircase leading into the drop room, where they placed a stepladder beside the suspended McGladdery and aided Dr Girvan as he established that life was extinct.

After every execution there was an inquest: a formality, of course, but necessary nonetheless. The 12-man jury in McGladdery's inquest, who were directed by

Dr Herbert P. Lowe, were there to consider the method of execution, the cause of death and the legality of the killing. To assist them in their deliberation, which by all accounts was not lengthy, a rather macabre document recording all aspects of the execution was completed by the prison's governor and the doctor in attendance.

In this document McGladdery was referred to only by his prison number 237/1961, and his weight was given as 152 pounds and his height as five feet nine-and-a-quarter inches. The executioner then set out first the length of the drop, which he had estimated before the execution, at five feet four inches, and then the drop which had taken place during the execution, measured from the level of the floor of the scaffold to the heels of the 'suspended culprit'. At five feet four-and-a-quarter inches, the actual drop was a mere quarter of an inch less than the estimate: a testament to the skill and accuracy of the hangman. As with most if not all executions by hanging, the cause of death was determined as dislocation of the vertebrae.

From there onwards, the execution record poses questions to both the governor and the doctor as to the suitability and capability of the executioner. First they are asked whether he had performed his duty satisfactorily and if his demeanour during his stay at the jail just before the execution was that of a respectable person. Next they are asked if they believed he was both mentally and physically fit to perform his duties, and if there was any possibility that he could discredit the process by reporting details about the execution to the press or others. Finally they are asked their opinion as to whether there were any reasons why he should not be employed in this capacity again. The document was little more than a job reference for Allen, but nevertheless was part of the submission to the inquest and afterwards filed among papers in the Ministry of Home Affairs at Stormont.

As was expected, the verdict of the inquest was 'death by judicial hanging', and the remains were prepared for burial in the confines of the prison's walls.

The body of Robert McGladdery was then taken in his pauper's coffin out through the passage beside the drop room and up a set of stone steps to the rear of C Wing to a place near the prison wall, where he was interred by a few hand-chosen inmates in an unmarked grave next to the body of that year's previous execution, Samuel McLaughlin. The inmates themselves often etched on the prison wall the names of the executed whom they had buried. That of Samuel McLaughlin and the year ''61' can clearly be seen scratched in the sandstone for anyone to see, but there is no marker for McGladdery. To this day his remains still lie beneath the gravel and concrete near the prison hospital, property of the state, until his remaining family decide to reclaim his body from what is now no longer a prison.

A few letters were sent from the condemned cell before Robert McGladdery's death, most of which only found their way to the addressees after the execution had taken place. Among those were two which were sent to his former Sunday school teacher. Most of the letters were brief and full of sentiment, and almost all relating to McGladdery's profession of faith in Jesus Christ and his having accepted the Lord as his Saviour. He even found time, on 18 December, to send his friend and drinking partner on the night of the murder, Will Copeland, a few lines in which he makes a half-hearted apology for attempting to implicate him at the trial a few months earlier, before informing him of his 'timely' conversion, all the time encouraging Copeland to seek the Lord for his own personal salvation.

I suspect that Will Copeland may have had one or two reservations as to whether McGladdery was serious or once again attempting to manipulate him in some way. His words were so simple and so naive. If his note to Copeland is to be taken literally, in McGladdery's eyes his past had just been wiped out, the slate well and truly clean simply because he had accepted that God existed. 'I haven't much time left Will, but now I believe in God and I believe I am going to Heaven I would like to meet you there.'

The threat of eternal damnation was undoubtedly a potent motive for his conversion, and it is fair to say that many, including myself, would remain sceptical about the timing. If Robert McGladdery had thought for one minute that he could cheat his way to paradise in the afterlife, I believe he would have tried his very best to do so. It is in our darkest hours that we reach out for comfort and hope. And there are many who find just that in religion and the belief in a merciful and forgiving God, their transgressions confessed and a penance accepted in return. But that contrition must be honest and heartfelt. Only McGladdery's God would know if that were the case.

On the same day of his execution the Reverend Vance, the chaplain who attended to Robert's spiritual needs right up until his final moments, wrote a short letter in which he stated that before the end McGladdery had 'accepted full responsibility' for Pearl Gamble's murder, as well as admitting to having burned the light blue suit which the police had looked for but never found. If those were McGladdery's actual words they fell well short of a full and frank confession. There was not going to be any eleventh-hour reprieve, and for the sake of his soul, and to ease the conscience of those around him who had played a part in his trial and conviction, he could have simply said that he had indeed murdered Pearl. In his own twisted way he may have even taken pleasure in leaving behind a small element of doubt.

Why he would have burned the suit rather than

secrete it along with the overcoat and shoes remains a mystery. One possible explanation is the fact that in order to get from the house to the septic tank he would have had to have worn some form of clothing and, as the suit was already dirty and contaminated, he would have worn it there and back and then burned it early the next morning. The bucket of black sludge recovered at the house during one of the searches may have been the remnants of that fire. But whatever the explanation, it hadn't made any difference to the outcome of the trial.

History was made on 20 December 1961, and McGladdery's name immortalised as that of the last man to be hanged in Northern Ireland. The abolitionists were close to achieving what they set out to do, with the last execution in Scotland taking place in 1963, and in England in 1964, when Harry Allen and Robert Stewart carried out the execution of two co-accused (Gwynne Evans and Peter Allen) simultaneously at two different locations in the country.

Over the next few years the condemned cell at Crumlin Road became obsolete and was used for various purposes, a storeroom for beds and blankets mostly, but never again to house inmates. However, one of the jail's most famous prisoners over the years, Augustus 'Gusty' Spence, did tell me that he had watched the 1966 World Cup Final on television in that particular cell, along with a few other prisoners.

But the execution room and the drop room fell into disrepair through lack of use, as a result of which the staircase was removed and the floor reinstated. The only reminder of their former role was the workings of the trapdoor which could be clearly seen if one stood below in the drop room. There was also a staircase situated in the middle of C Wing which led down into the chamber containing the drop room and the other three original punishment cells, and this too was eventually closed off and covered over by heather-brown floor tiles in keeping with the rest of the wing.

That particular episode in the history of the jail was shut away and forgotten for many years afterwards, until the jail itself finally closed its doors to inmates in 1996.

As Northern Ireland moved through darker times and eventually entered a more stable and more democratic political era, interest in securing and preserving certain aspects of our past became issues which were being tabled for discussion. Crumlin Road Prison was a place rich in history, and not just in relation to political events and people involved in the Troubles of the period from 1969 until the 1990s. The jail and its inhabitants had been described over the years as being a microcosm of society on the outside, with its population rising and falling in response to social deprivation or political unrest at the time.

Thousands of men, women and children had been incarcerated over the 150 years or so since its doors had been opened for business, and it had seen countless deaths and births over that time.

For those reasons alone, as well as the fact that the building is a fine example of functional Victorian architecture, the idea of opening the jail as a tourist attraction was considered and eventually implemented during 2007. Of course, one of the main attractions of the limited tour on offer is a visit to the condemned cell, the execution room and the drop room. These have been restored as sympathetically as possible, and to add to the experience, one of the two executioners' boxes containing the tools of his trade, including the noose which was likely used during McGladdery's execution, are there to see.

Some may regard this aspect of the tour ghoulish, but I find it fascinating to be able to experience some of the atmosphere of events which, although they seem light-years away from the criminal justice system of today, remain in living memory for many of us.

CHAPTER ELEVEN
MURDER TRAIL

Throughout the process of researching and writing this book, as I pored over document after document, newspaper clipping and microfiche roll, as well as talking to those old enough to remember the incident well, I realised that I was being drawn closer to the characters about whom I was writing, in particular to Pearl Gamble herself. A three-dimensional picture had began to form in my mind of a living, breathing Pearl, her bones fleshed out by the descriptions given by her family and friends, and all her little traits and foibles, right down to her sense of style, recreating this very real and vibrant teenager. The more I learned about her the more I was sure she was someone I would have liked. It took me by surprise in many ways, as I was determined to remain objective during the writing process, but I was developing a genuine affection for her, and consequently a loathing for the man who had taken her life. I can only liken it to the fondness a writer of fiction often develops for the hero or heroine they have created: a character they have written into existence and who most often has a likeable persona, in stark contrast to the dark and sinister nature of the villain. Unfortunately, there is no fictional element to this story, even though the events related here seem as if they might have come straight from the pages of a crime novel.

In this book at least, Pearl is in many ways my heroine, although the tragedy that befalls her always threatens to overshadow the true story of this inspirational young woman. It was her love of life, and of those with whom she shared her 19 years, which gave her the strength not to give up but instead to fight her attacker with every ounce of her being until she could fight no more. A gentle and loving soul growing up in a happy family environment, Pearl could never have imagined that she would be caught up in the twisted fantasy of a violent and disturbed man such as Robert McGladdery. It is difficult to understand just how two people who had come from very similar social backgrounds, growing up in the same rural area and even sharing a tenuous family link, could have ended up complete opposites in terms of their natures.

The legacy McGladdery left behind was one of strife and heartbreak, and not just for the remaining members of Pearl's family. In a little rural town such as Newry, it must have been difficult for Agnes McGladdery and her remaining sons and daughters to continue to live normal lives, always aware of the negativity surrounding their name. A friend of mine who had grown up in the town during the late Fifties and early Sixties remembered Mrs McGladdery working in a little shop in Sugar Island, close to the town hall. She described her as a nervous little woman, very polite and accommodating, but with what appeared to be the troubles of the world weighing heavily on her shoulders.

The stigma attached to being part of the family of Robert McGladdery, the cold-blooded murderer, was something which would have been difficult to come to terms with, even more so in such a parochial little area of Northern Ireland, and in much simpler times. I can fully understand how his siblings would have tried to distance themselves from it at every opportunity. But we must all accept that we have no control over the actions of others, regardless of their being family or friends, and as individuals we carve out our own path in life as best we can. Robert McGladdery chose his own way and, by his own admission in his 'autobiography', he was 'the black sheep' of his family.

Yet again we must consider that Pearl, who

undoubtedly paid the ultimate price on 28 January 1961, was not the only victim of the events of that night, for there were many more.

I knew roughly where, at that time, the Upper Damolly crossroads would have been in relation to the main Belfast Road in Newry and, on a slightly overcast day in June 2008, I set out to find the spot where my heroine had lost her young life. On approaching the town I turned left on to the Upper Damolly Road and carried on past hedgerow after hedgerow, further into the rolling hills of County Down. I was a little apprehensive as I drove along this road, which was barely able to take the width of two cars, fearing the passage of time would have changed the features of the landscape beyond recognition, and any chance of finding the places referred to in statements and depositions would be slim. All the way down from Loughbrickland, travelling towards the Sheep Bridge Inn and Tinkers Hill, I had encountered new road layouts, with sprawling bungalows and houses dotted along either side of the carriageway. Newry and the countryside beyond did not appear to have suffered from any lack of prosperity. Over a period of years the 'frontier' town had witnessed an upsurge in shoppers from the Republic travelling north of the border in an attempt to combat rising consumer prices in the South brought on by the ravenous 'Celtic tiger' economy.

Newry had in some ways undergone a gold rush, and looked all the healthier for it.

The first junction I came to was not what I would have described as a crossroads, although its position on the map I had drawn up would have been about correct. On my right I was aware that another, nameless thoroughfare was merging at the edge of the Damolly Road, but directly opposite it on my left was what appeared to be a concrete lane leading up and over a steep rise. I continued on for about another hundred yards, but something made me turn around and drive back along to the concrete lane and turn on to it. When I drove up this and crested the top of the hill, there, further along on my left, was a small worker's cottage, and I knew instantly that I was looking at the house where Pearl Gamble had grown up.

As I turned around and looked back towards the crossroads, every little detail began to fall into place. The road opposite where I stood, itself a steep incline rising steadily from the crossroads below, was Primrose Hill, and the field to the right of that was where the first real signs of Pearl's struggle with her attacker came to light.

Almost directly opposite the Gambles' house was a large farmhouse, a hive of activity as vehicles moved up and down the lane, back and forward into the yard beyond. The farm buildings looked as though they had been around as long as the cottage had, and in an attempt to ascertain ownership of the fields across the way, I called at the door and spoke with the man of the house. A farmer's time is precious, I know, and at first he was slightly annoyed at this interruption to his well-earned morning cup of tea. But as soon as he knew the nature of my visit, and the conversation got around to the Gambles' house and the events of 1961, he was happy to stand a while longer and share his memories with me. He was only a young boy when the murder took place, and on the day of Pearl's disappearance was in his sick bed upstairs in the main house and was looking out across the fields, where he could see several policemen standing at the gap in the hedge beside Primrose Hill. Because of his age he wasn't really aware of what was going on at the time but, as he grew up, the story was told to him again and again by his parents and other family members, to the point where he knew almost everything there was to know about how and where McGladdery had lain in wait for his victim.

There was another reason why the story was so engrained in his mind, though, for his family had purchased the cottage that the Gambles had lived in when Pearl's parents and siblings had moved out after their daughter's death, and it still remained in the family. Not many years later, about 1963 or 1964, tragedy again visited the little house, when his uncle, who was living there at the time, drowned along with two other wildfowlers while out shooting ducks in a local lough. According to him, the cottage had not changed in any way since the Sixties, save, of course, for the satellite dish now attached to the front wall. From the greying slates on the roof to the little return at the back which was likely to have housed the outside toilet, it looked like hundreds of other little cottages up and down the country.

As I stood looking at it I tried to imagine Pearl, her brother and sisters and her parents all living under that same little roof, continually bumping into one another and vying for what little privacy they could get. At that time it wasn't an unusual situation for so many to live together. There just weren't as many houses available as there are today, and with courting couples tending to wait until marriage before setting up home together, young men and women remained with their parents for much longer, often into their thirties.

Having gained permission to cross into the fields at Primrose Hill, I made my way down towards the crossroads. As I reached the junction I couldn't help but feel frustration as I realised just how close to being in the safety of her home Pearl had been when she stepped from the car and bid her friends good night. She had been less than 200 yards from her own front door when McGladdery had accosted her on the road.

Had she tried to cry out when she was first attacked? And even if she had, would anyone have heard her? As she was being punched and kicked, and pushed further up the road towards the gap in the hedge, she must have been able to see the moonlight reflecting off the gable end of the little cottage, her sanctuary slowly slipping beyond her reach as she tried to pull away from his relentless onslaught.

The greying clouds above me now rolled ominously from the direction of Carlingford Lough, the air filled with the threat of rain as I moved up the field towards the gap in the hedge at the top of the hill. Even on a day like this, anyone moving through this area would be visible for quite a distance. But on a dark January night some 50 years ago, in the very early hours, nobody was there to witness the two figures struggling from one field into the next. Even now the area still seems so remote, with only a handful of more recent houses having been built on the footprint of existing settlements.

The view from the top of the hill as I walked into the tall grass beyond the gap in the hedge was spectacular. All around cattle grazed in a patchwork of fields or wandered among clumps of gorse as the backdrop of the mountains framed the picturesque landscape. But as I stood for a moment to get my bearings in relation to the site of Weir's Rocks, I felt slightly uneasy. The breeze played across the top of the grass as if to open a pathway in front of me, and the branches from an oak which stood alone in the centre of the field seemed to murmur as they rocked gently from side to side. To my right, about a quarter of a mile away, I could make out an outcrop of rocks speckled among the explosive yellow flowers of the gorse, a desolate spot where I imagined few people ever ventured. It was the place where Robert McGladdery had dragged Pearl Gamble's broken body and then dumped her in the tangled undergrowth, and for some reason I did not want to go any further. There was little to achieve by going on other than to retrace the killer's steps, and I already knew that Pearl had died somewhere close to where I was now standing. I could feel it.

This innocuous piece of farmland I was standing on I knew meant little, if anything at all, to the many people who passed by it every day. But for me, having read and reread every detail about the events of the morning of 28 January 1961, and having become deeply involved in Pearl's story, it was like visiting an important historical site. It was just as atmospheric and as haunting as any battlefield or castle rampart. For me it was a special place, not in a ghoulish sense, but in the way that the world had seemed to move on around it while it remained very much untouched, preserved almost, as any place of interest should be.

Arguably the whole story of Pearl's murder is a part of

Newry's history, its social history at least, just as any other event which had a profound effect on the community would be considered. But I wasn't so naive as to have expected a signpost or marker pointing out the 'McGladdery tourist trail'. I could see just how raw the emotions could still be even so many years later. But what I had found at the Upper Damolly crossroads was more than I could have hoped for, regardless of whether it had been maintained unwittingly. It didn't just stop there, though, and less than ten minutes later I was again transported back in time as I stopped my car just a few doors from 4 Damolly Terrace, the house where Robert McGladdery had lived with his mother.

When you leave the main Belfast Road and turn into Ardmore, heading towards Damolly, the modern bungalows and wide tarmac surfaces are in keeping with the image of Newry as a modern city. After 100 yards or so the road bends round to the right, skirting a bank on the left which falls away into a field below, and almost immediately you come upon a breathtaking row of stone-built terraced houses abutting the pavement on the right. Without the numerous cars parked outside, the UPVC double glazing and the odd satellite dish, the houses could have looked just as they had done half a century before. Sitting across from them all on its own was a small white commercial property displaying a sign declaring it to be a hairdressing salon. It took very little imagination to recreate it as the local village shop, and that is exactly what it had been in its former life. Back in the Sixties the little shop had been McGuigan's, which would have served practically all of the village community and those making their way to and from the Damolly Mill. It was also where folk would have dropped off their shoes for repair, having been unable to raise McGladdery from his bed.

This was just as exciting a find as the one I had just come from at the Upper Damolly crossroads, but although I was naturally curious about one particular house in the row, I couldn't help but be impressed by all the houses and how sympathetically they had been maintained. For a few minutes or so I poked around at the bottom of the street, all the time being watched by a grey-haired man who had been standing in his doorway taking the morning sun. Finally curiosity got the better of me and I approached him and introduced myself, expecting a short conversation when I told him of my interests. I couldn't have been more wrong. This man had lived all of his life, some 60-odd years, in the same house, and had grown up knowing Robert McGladdery. As we stood and chatted I could sense his enthusiasm, the story of Pearl Gamble's murder clearly being one that he had told many times before. But the version he had grown up with, although close to the truth, had evolved slightly, taking on the odd embellishment as it went. In fairness to my friend, though, he was not alone in that aspect.

Each of the few locals I had spoken to had added to the story a piece which I knew was inaccurate or just pure fantasy, one even suggesting that McGladdery had been chased by the police for some three months before he was eventually caught.

Still, it was interesting talking with someone who had lived beside and played with the young Robbie, and remembered above all else that he was a young man filled with anger and rage, and that it had been no surprise to anyone, least of all those who knew him well, that he had murdered Pearl. As we stood there swapping information, he told me a particular story about an evening when McGladdery had gone to Banbridge, a small town just to the north of Newry, for a night out in the pubs. As the story goes, a certain character from Banbridge had chosen that evening to stake his claim as the town's leading thug, and in a certain pub had produced a knife from his coat pocket and stuck it into the wooden counter-top, stating, 'I'm the hardest man in Banbridge, and don't anyone forget it!'

According to the legend, McGladdery sidled up to the bar beside him, produced a hatchet from under his coat and drove it into the wooden surface next to the knife, looked him in the eye and said, 'Well, I'm Robert McGladdery, and I'm the hardest man in Newry and

Banbridge!' The other man backed away and McGladdery continued on drinking.

There are many such tales about the man, and most have little if any truth to them, but there is no doubt that he had built a reputation for himself, and one which made him recognisable to a lot of people, both young and old, living in and around his home town.

I remember reading on the internet excerpts from the memories of a man who had started his working career in the Civil Service in Newry in the late Fifties. In his writings he recalls McGladdery, describing him as 'a tall, blond, good looking chap. He was also a bit of a thug who was often involved in fights at dances etc.' He also remembered the rumour that McGladdery was said to carry a hatchet around with him, and recalled seeing him standing at the entrance to the market, which was right across the street from the office he worked in, 'flipping a knife'.

It is understandable that, in the aftermath of the murder, this image of McGladdery loitering in the street while toying with a knife in his hand is one which would have stuck in that author's mind. There was always a dark and sinister side to McGladdery, and he was clearly used to and comfortable with his renown as a man of violence. He exuded menace, and many who knew him must have thought that it would only be a matter of time before he would push his luck too far.

After about 20 minutes or so chatting with my friend at the front door of his house, I said my goodbyes and headed back towards my car. The day had brightened somewhat, blue skies forming the backdrop to the row of terraces which looked down towards the Clanrye River as it slowly made its way down towards Carlingford Lough, passing through flat green fields before edging anonymously through the streets and car parks of Newry itself. A few hundred yards or so from the bottom of the terrace, just a little further down the road, in an area covered by lush green trees, stood the now abandoned site of the Damolly Mill, the workplace of Agnes McGladdery and two of Pearl's sisters at the time of the murder.

The view across the meadow towards Camlough mountain, with the extinct volcano of Slieve Gullion just to the south, was blissful and serene, interrupted only occasionally by the sound of one or two cars passing along the road behind me, and I couldn't help but wonder if that beauty was ever something which Robert McGladdery either contemplated or appreciated as he stepped out of the front door of his house on his way to meet friends or just walk into town. It may sound rather simplistic but although I know that McGladdery was leading anything but the high life, scratching a living from the odd shoe-mending job and whatever he got from his little criminal enterprises, I believe he was rich in terms of where he was living and what was around him. It is true that we can all be guilty of taking our surroundings for granted, never appreciating how others may look upon our situation as idyllic, but as I watched the sun come out from behind a cloud and spill on to the pastoral scene below me, I knew that McGladdery must have been wholly different from the vast majority of us if his soul was never touched by this vista. To live with this constant beauty every day, whether a divine creation or an evolutionary masterpiece, and yet harbour such dark and menacing thoughts inside suggests a deeply troubled mind.

No one could ever accuse me of being timid or retiring, but the idea of knocking on the door of 4 Damolly Terrace and speaking to the occupant filled me with apprehension. I did not want to invade anyone's privacy, but my friend from further down the terrace whom I had spoken to earlier had assured me that the woman who lived there was more than approachable. All the same, I tapped on the little glass pane with all the temerity of a schoolboy wanting to retrieve his ball from a neighbour's back garden. The door was opened a few moments later by a strong, confident redhead, who I am sure would not mind if I described her as a woman rather than a girl. I had no idea how to start the conversation other than to ask if she knew that she now lived in a house which had a certain history attached to it. It was a question I knew the answer to just as soon as I saw the reaction on her face.

It would have been easy to fall in love with such a house, simply from looking at the outside alone. The stone walls and the brightly painted window frames of the neighbouring properties in the terrace all serve to create a sense of character, and there is an obvious pride in ownership. That and the enviable view from the front windows were what drew the current owner to buy the property just a few years ago, completely unaware of the significance of one of its previous tenants, that is until the very day she was signing for the purchase. With her mind already made up, and after a little reassurance from a local clergyman who visited the house a short time later, there were no regrets. There were no ghosts haunting this house, no cold spots or malevolent presences, and no bad luck attached to living here. This was merely where Robert Andrew McGladdery had lived for some years, and it was only that fact, and that fact alone, which made number four stand out among the rest of the cottages in this picturesque little row.

But there was one coincidence which I found astounding when this woman recounted it to me as I stood outside her door. In her previous job in the offices of a local Justice of the Peace she had been encouraged by her employer to meet one particular female client who was there to attend to paperwork concerning a recently deceased relative. The woman in question had made the trip from England and was in the office for no more than a few minutes. The two women were introduced, and only after divulging her address as 4 Damolly Terrace was she told that she was speaking to one of Pearl Gamble's sisters. It was an address that this visitor to the town could never forget, and nor could any other member of her family, for obvious reasons, and she simply said, 'Yes, that is where McGladdery lived.'

Even though I am sure I won't be the last person ever to stand and stare at her front door, I know that the current owner of the cottage will not mind in the slightest. In this tranquil little haven a few minutes from a busy town centre she enjoys peace and quiet in abundance, and in the short time that she has lived there she has stamped her own identity on the house. It may always be associated with Robert McGladdery, but only in the sense that it helps map out for people like me the geography of the event.

As I walked away from the terrace towards the Belfast Road, which leads into Newry, I looked down into the field below me on the right, searching for a gap in the hedge. Somewhere about here, close to this side of the field, was the septic tank where McGladdery had hidden the bloodstained clothes after the murder. Just before I reached the boundary wall of a sprawling newly built house I came upon a lane leading down towards the field, and when I had walked its length I found myself standing only yards from the septic tank. There was no doubt in my mind that it was the very same one. Its location was exactly where it had been described by Detective Sergeant Jeffrey, and must have been close to the 376 paces he had measured out between it and 4 Damolly Terrace. If McGladdery had not drawn any attention to that area on the evening of 9 February 1961 his hiding place could have remained undiscovered. That and some luck provided the evidence which sealed his fate during the trial, lending much-needed substance to the prosecution's heavily circumstantial case. It was a fairly nondescript find in that it was a simple, concrete-covered septic tank, but it was yet another element of the story, and a fairly important one at that, virtually unchanged all these years later.

It is one thing to research an event and create a picture in your mind's eye of the places concerned, but to actually see those places in very much the same condition as they would have been is remarkable, and in many ways helps you to sense the atmosphere.

As I drove through Newry I recognised other locations that related to the case, in particular the site of the Orange Hall on the Belfast Road just alongside the telephone exchange. But there was one place I felt that I needed to visit out of respect more than anything else.

The tiny little graveyard at Meeting House Green sits

well below street level at the top of Church Street, out of sight and in most cases out of mind to those living around the area. To get there you have to descend a number of stone steps and then negotiate an iron gate at the bottom. The steps appear to be well used, but I know that this is due more to the graveyard's being somewhat of a shortcut between Windmill Road and Church Street rather than to the frequent footfalls of relatives of the deceased buried there. Most of the graves appear overgrown and unkempt, with many headstones damaged and in need of repair. Her grave wasn't hard to find at all, as it was almost immediately on my right as I passed through the gate and stepped on to a gravel path. It stood out from the plots around it, as the majority of them were obviously a lot older, many dating back to the late 19th century and the very early part of the 20th. The headstone was simple and plain, and the inscription did not allude to the manner of her departure, stating only that it had been erected by her friends in her memory. Sadly there are now two additions to the plot, whose names appear below Pearl's: those of her father Robert, who died in May 1973, and her mother Margaret, who survived until 1986, living well into her eighties.

Beside the grave I found a small spray of dried and withered flowers, and, sitting on the plinth beneath the granite stone, a tray containing imitation violets. I suspect that there are frequent enough visitors who pay their respects here, and not just Pearl's remaining immediate family. For those who continued to live in Newry after everything that took place that year, and particularly for her close friends, this quiet little graveyard may have been the only place where they could come to escape the changes happening around them. They would have remembered Pearl exactly as she was the last time they laid eyes on her, youthful and full of hope for the future, and in doing so may themselves have been able to recapture the essence of the times they too enjoyed before her passing marked the end of an innocence.